Harwood Fundamentals of Pure and Applied Economics

MARXISM AND "REALLY EXISTING SOCIALISM"

Routledge
Taylor & Francis Group
LONDON AND NEW YORK

MARXIAN ECONOMICS II
In 3 Volumes

MARXISM AND "REALLY EXISTING SOCIALISM"

ALEC NOVE

Routledge
Taylor & Francis Group
LONDON AND NEW YORK

First published in 1986 by
Harwood Academic Publishers GmbH

Reprinted in 2001 by
Routledge
2 Park Square, Milton Park, Abingdon, Oxon, OX14 4RN

Simultaneously published in the USA and Canada by Routledge

711 Third Avenue, New York, NY 10017

Transferred to Digital Printing 2007

Routledge is an imprint of the Taylor & Francis Group, an informa business

First issued in paperback 2013

British Library Cataloguing in Publication Data
A CIP catalogue record for this book
is available from the British Library

Marxism and "Really Existing Socialism"

ISBN 978-0-415-26988-9 (hbk)
ISBN 978-0-415-86614-9 (pbk)

Marxism and "Really Existing Socialism"

Alec Nove
University of Glasgow, Scotland

A volume in the Marxian Economics section
edited by
John E. Roemer
University of California, Davis, USA

harwood academic publishers
chur · london · paris · new york

Harwood Academic Publishers

P.O. Box 197
London WC2E 9PX
England

58, rue Lhomond
75005 Paris
France

P.O. Box 786
Cooper Station
New York, NY 10276
United States of America

Library of Congress Cataloging-in-Publication Data

Nove, Alec.
Marxism and "really existing socialism."

(Fundamentals of pure and applied economics; v. 8
Marxian economics section)
Includes index.
1. Marxian economics. 2. Communism—Soviet Union.
3. Radicalism. I. Title. II. Series: Fundamentals of
pure and applied economics; v. 8. III. Series:
Fundamentals of pure and applied economics. Marxian
economics section.
HB97.5.N598 1986 335.4 86-14939
ISBN 3-7186-0330-6

ISBN 3 7186-0330-6. ISSN 0191-1708.

Contents

Introduction to the Series

Drawing on a personal network, an economist can still relatively easily stay well informed in the narrow field in which he works, but to keep up with the development of economics as a whole is a much more formidable challenge. Economists are confronted with difficulties associated with the rapid development of their discipline. There is a risk of "balkanisation" in economics, which may not be favorable to its development.

Fundamentals of Pure and Applied Economics has been created to meet this problem. The discipline of economics has been subdivided into sections (listed inside). These sections include short books, each surveying the state of the art in a given area.

Each book starts with the basic elements and goes as far as the most advanced results. Each should be useful to professors needing material for lectures, to graduate students looking for a global view of a particular subject, to professional economists wishing to keep up with the development of their science, and to researchers seeking convenient information on questions that incidentally appear in their work.

Each book is thus a presentation of the state of the art in a particular field rather than a step-by-step analysis of the development of the literature. Each is a high-level presentation but accessible to anyone with a solid background in economics, whether engaged in business, government, international organizations, teaching, or research in related fields.

Three aspects of *Fundamentals of Pure and Applied Economics* should be emphasized:

—First, the project covers the whole field of economics, not only theoretical or mathematical economics.

—Second, the project is open-ended and the number of books is not predetermined. If new interesting areas appear, they will generate additional books.
—Last, all the books making up each section will later be grouped to constitute one or several volumes of an Encyclopedia of Economics.

The editors of the sections are outstanding economists who have selected as authors for the series some of the finest specialists in the world.

J. Lesourne *H. Sonnenschein*

Marxism and "Really Existing Socialism"

ALEC NOVE

University of Glasgow, Scotland

1. CRITERIA

What is the connection between the Soviet system, as developed under Stalin and as modified since his death, and the socialism envisaged by Marx? That there are differences is, of course, both obvious and inevitable, and this for several reasons. Firstly, Marx nowhere systematically set out any "blueprint" of a socialist future, and indeed considered such exercises to be futile and even reactionary. His refusal to give any detailed description of a future world was no doubt part of his sincere conviction that *his* ideas on socialism were quite distinct from those whom he called utopian socialists. Secondly, Marx has been dead for over a hundred years, and even his most fervent and uncritical admirers would agree that this great man could not foresee all that was to come, computers to nuclear weapons included. Quite evidently he would have modified his doctrines in the light of experience, including the experience of socialist planning. Thirdly, since he could not modify his doctrines after his death, we must, unless we are uncurable dogmatist believers, perform this task ourselves: which of Marx's ideas on socialism appear to be contradictory or unreal, given the experience of "really existing socialism"? Only then might it be possible to develop a critique of such socialism in marxist terms. To take a simple example, there is in Marx the belief that under socialism the division of labour will be transcended (*aufgehoben*). In the USSR the reverse has been the case, in respect both of the horizontal (specialization, professionalization) and the vertical (hierarchical) division of labour. How far, we may ask, was this development the inescapable consequence of industrial development under state auspices, and, if so, does this not provide a basis for a criticism of Marx rather than of Soviet practice?

This brings me to the heart of the whole question of appropriate criteria, in judging both Soviet reality and the validity of marxian doctrine. To take another example to which we will return, what does Soviet experience tell us about the validity of the doctrine of historical materialism? In the introduction to my *Economic History of the USSR,* I quoted Lenin: "Politics cannot but have dominance over economics: to argue otherwise is to forget the ABC of Marxism". A Soviet critic cited that passage, and accused me (not unfairly) of omitting a subsequent passage in which Lenin spoke of "politics as concentrated economics" [39, p. 21]. Of course the two are closely linked, particularly where the state owns and manages the economy, but to interpret Russian history since 1917 in terms of any species of economic determinism (even "in the last instance") really does require an illegitimate leap of imagination—at least in my opinion.

But let us look first at how "socialism" or "communism" was understood by Marx and Engels, and by marxists of the post-Stalin period.

Marx himself made no clear distinction between "socialism" and "communism", and the notion that one was the lower stage of the other first made its appearance after the Russian revolution (it was *not* an invention of Stalin. Bukharin, Trotsky, Preobrazhensky used such phrases too). Of course, Marx appreciated that full socialism/communism would not appear overnight, that there would be a transition period, a lower stage—of which more in a moment. However, socialism and communism for him were virtually synonyms, to be used interchangeably.

Let me briefly (too briefly?) set out what Marx's vision contained. Probably the most thorough collection of its contents, with appropriate references, is to be found in Bertil Ollman's article, in *Critique,* n° 8. The key elements were:

a) *Abundance.* Capitalism has at least potentially overcome the problem of creating a sufficiency of productive potential to meet all reasonable needs. Capitalist relations of production are acting as a brake on the development of productive forces.

Remove that brake, and production and productivity would rapidly increase. It is on this basis that we will see the end of acquisitiveness, selfishness, the struggle of each against each. Attempts to create socialism amid relative poverty would reproduce "the old rubbish".

b) *Overcoming "commodity fetishism" and the market.* Private property in means of production, the separation of production units from each other, requires ex post validation of the value of commodities through the process of sale and exchange, through the market. The relationship between men takes the form of relationship between things. Under socialism, labour power will be applied directly by the "associated producers" to the tasks of satisfying society's needs for goods and services. It will be possible to calculate the number of hours of human effort required, and to relate this to the social utility of what is produced, without a detour via exchange-value and the market. "There can be nothing more erroneous and absurd than to postulate the control by united individuals of total production on the basis of exchange value, of money" [34, pp. 138–9].

c) *Elimination of the wages system and of money.* Since calculations of cost are to be in labour-time, and there will be no purchase-and-sale, money will wither away as a medium of exchange. Under fully-developed socialism/communism there will be realised the aim of "from each according to their abilities, to each according to their needs". In the transition period, however, when people's consciousness is not yet fully socialist (and abundance is not yet achieved), people will be "paid" according to their work. It is not clear if work is to be measured in hours, or whether differential rewards are envisaged for work of different quality or intensity. In any case, pay will not be in money but in non-circulating tokens, presumably denominated in hours and minutes.

d) *Elimination of the division of labour and of alienation.* Educated, all-purpose human beings will interchange jobs. There will be no need for hierarchy, or where it is needed the task of coordination/command can be taken in turn. The causes of alienation will be overcome. There will be no professional bureaucracy, officers, etc.

e) *The withering away of the state.* The state being essentially an organ of class oppression will no longer have any purpose. Since there will be no class conflict, no special repressive machine will be needed, therefore laws, judges, police, become unnecessary.
f) *Planning,* undertaken in the advance knowledge of needs and of available means, will be a simple matter. It is the market, the separation of producters from the product and from each other, that makes it all so complicated. There will be a huge saving arising out of the waste (*faux-frais*) in the circulatory sphere, which Marx treated as unproductive.
g) *The proletariat,* in liberating itself, will end class oppression and bring into being a classless society.

As is clear from successive versions of his reply to Vera Zasulich, Marx took very seriously the notion of a primitive communist society that once existed, in which there was an organic fusion of the individual with society. (Whether there ever was such a society is a question I will not discuss.) His socialism/communism involves a restoration of this organic fusion, but of course on the basis of the highest modern technique and the full development of the productive forces. This explains, as Agnes Heller has rightly pointed out, why Marx devoted no attention to the rather vital questions of how decisions are to be taken (on the economy or on anything else) and how differences of view are to be reconciled: "there will . . . be no group interest or conflict of interests" [21 p. 130].

Already at this stage the attentive reader will have noted this author's belief that Marxian socialism and "really existing socialism" diverge largely, but certainly not exclusively, because of the utopian-romantic aspects of Marx's vision. Utopian visions have their important role to play, in inspiring action and sacrifice. But by definition they are unrealisable, and this renders those who fail to realise them immune from the criticism of not having achieved the impossible. But let us now look at the socialist ideas of marxists after Marx, and before Soviet experience could have taught any lessons.

August Bebel had worked closely with Engels, and, though not himself an intellectual "heavyweight", can be seen as representative of much social-democratic opinion in pre-1914 Germany, a time when the party was considered to be orthodox-marxist in its ideological stance. For some reason the most systematic exposition of his view on socialist planning is to be found in his *Woman under socialism* (*Die Frau im Sozialismus*).

The complexities of real planning in a modern industrial society was not understood by him. Such phrases as "child's play", the belief that socialist man would take the needed decisions on the basis of readily-available information, anticipate similar statements by Russian revolutionary theorists, which will be cited in a moment. Clearly Bebel derived from Marx and Engels the belief that a classless, socially coherent society will be one without conflict over resource allocation. To cite Bebel again: "The gratification of personal egoism and the promotion of the common weal go harmoniously hand in hand and coincide".

Kautsky was another of the associates of Engels in his last years, and more of a theorist than Bebel, with whom he collaborated closely. It is not clear whether he ever read, or took seriously, Enrico Barone's pioneering work on "The ministry of production in a collectivist state", which was published in 1908 and put highly pertinent questions about how calculations could be made in an imaginary socialist commonwealth. Kautsky also envisaged a socialism without markets, which led him to envisage a number of relatively autarkic socialist societies (since it would be necessary to keep *trade* to a minimum). True, he specifically disavowed utopias, and, in one of his works (*Die soziale Revolution*) envisaged the use of prices in the "circuit of commodities". Oskar Lange saw in this an important contribution to economic theories of socialism, but since Kautsky imagined that price ratios "historically given" (i.e. derived from the capitalist past) would be used, it really does not seem that he saw any active allocative role for prices. Acknowledgments are due to T. Kowalik and P. Sutela for drawing attention to these aspects of Kautsky's thoughts. And in his article on the Erfurt programme Kautsky wrote that "in a socialist society, which is after all just a single giant industrial enterprise, production and wages must be organized in a planned way, like in a modern large industrial enterprise". The reference to "wages" is interesting: it implies money, though Kautsky did not enlarge on this point. His notion of socialist economy as one gigantic enterprise does have some marxian roots, and, as we shall see, Lenin saw things this way too. But Kautsky was committed to parliamentary democracy, as the political way towards achieving socialism under conditions of universal suffrage, and on this issue he clashed very sharply with Lenin after the Bolshevik seizure of power.

Lenin's pre-1918 ideas on the economics and politics of socialism should be well known, and it may therefore be unnecessary to dwell on them for long. The following would seem to be the key elements in the present context. *Firstly,* there is his concept of the role of the revolutionary intelligentsia in bringing specifically socialist ideas to the working class which, left to itself, would not go beyond "trade unionism", i.e. demands for economic betterment. Thus they would seek higher wages, not the abolition of capitalism and of the wages system as such. While Lenin was criticised by Rosa Luxemburg, who had a greater belief in the virtues of working-class spontaneity, it has been pointed out (notably by Harding [20]) that similar ideas had been expressed by both Kautsky and the menshevik theorist Axelrod. *Secondly,* there was Lenin's concept of the party. Here again it is noteworthy that Plekhanov at first took his side, and it may well be that the disciplined, conspiratorial elite concept was largely the result of the peculiar circumstances of Tsarist Russia. It will be necessary to trace the route by which this concept of the party became the rather different notion of the one-party state. Just as Lenin's well-known article on "party literature", which when it was written (in 1905) referred to the duties of party members in a situation when there were other parties and other literatures, became a justification for imposing *partiinost'* on everybody. But this is to run ahead. His authoritarian concept of the party was linked with a very strong emphasis on the *dictatorial* aspect of the "dictatorship of the proletariat".

The *third* element of Lenin's ideas was the oddly libertarian politics which are to be found in *State and Revolution,* which contrast strangely with the authoritarian Lenin. He imagined that everyone will be able to run their own affairs "without compulsion, without subordination, without that special *apparatus* for compulsion which is called the state". In the *State and Revolution,* surprisingly, the Party is not even mentioned. Oddly enough, he cited, in that same work, Engels's remark to the effect that "wanting to abolish authority in large-scale industry is tantamount to wanting to abolish industry itself". Yet here, and in such works as "Will the Bolsheviks retain state power" and "The coming catastrophe", he insisted that capitalism had "so simplified" the organization and planning of production and distribution that any literate and numerate person can perform these functions in turn. "To organize the whole economy on the lines of the postal service, all under the leadership of the armed workers, that is our immediate (*sic*) task", he wrote in *State and Revolution,* in 1917. Like Kautsky before him, he imagined socialist industry as a kind of huge single enterprise, managed somehow by society as a whole. His study of the German war economy convinced him that if the Kaiser's government could control the economy and the big cartels, so could a proletarian government. So a *fourth* characteristic of Lenin's view of socialism is (following Marx) a gross oversimplification of the task of planning, a lack of any grasp of economic problems, as distinct from those of engineering and accountancy. He was quick to learn, but there was much he had to learn.

Bukharin had attended lectures in economics in Vienna. But he too, both in the *ABC of Communism* which he wrote with Preobrazhensky, and in his *Economics of the Transition Period* [8], seemed blissfully unaware of *economic* problems under a future socialism. "The factories, workshops, mines and other productive institutions will all be subdivisions, as it were, of one vast people's workshop, which will embrace the entire national economy of production". This means that "everything must be precisely calculated. We must know in advance how much labour to assign to the various branches of industry; what products are required and how much of each it is necessary to produce; how and where machines must be provided . . . The communist system of production presupposes in addition that production is not for the market, but for use . . . The work of production will be effected by the giant cooperative as a whole. In consequence of this change, we will no longer have *commodities,* only *products.* These products are not exchanged for one another; they are neither bought nor sold"—and so on [6, pp. 114, 116]. Money is to wither away. Such ideas as these were typical of the Bolshevik party outlook in the period of 1917–20, and found their reflection in the party programme adopted in 1919.

Of course what was actually going on during the period of so-called war communism was vastly different. The peasants were subject to requisitioning, a centralized authoritarian system allocated resources, representative bodies (soviets, trade unions) were placed firmly under party control or were simply dissolved. It seemed to many at the time and since that this was due to dire emergency. But some important features of "war communism" were the result of ideological fervour and illusions, as several of the protagonists were later to admit. Thus hyper-inflation was greeted by some comrades, Preobrazhensky for instance, as a positive step in the desired elimination of money on the road to communism. And Trotsky defended militarization of labour not just as a necessary emergency expedient, but as an integral part of the whole transition period to communism, when the higher consciousness of the workers would make compulsion unnecessary, and Bukharin agreed with him.

By the time the civil war was won, thousands of party officials had become accustomed to the brutal exercise of power, to arrests of all and any political opponents, to requisitioning and terror. Many were dismayed by the adoption by the 10th party congress of policies which became known as NEP (indeed, the full implications of NEP did not become clear until some months after the congress). It was recognised that this represented, in Bukharin's words, "the collapse of our illusions". A compromise proved necessary with the hated petty-bourgeoisie. Lenin called it a "retreat". No one equated NEP and socialism. When, in 1925, the Stalin–Bukharin majority put forward the slogan of "socialism in one country" it was presented as a realisable aim, not as an attained reality. Even Trotsky found it hard, until after his exile, to deny the possibility of "building" socialism in Russia.

It was Zinoviev in particular who denounced the notion of "socialism in one country" as doctrinal heresy. At least until after his exile, Trotsky was more ambiguous. True, they had hoped for world revolution. It had not happened. Russia stood alone. But it was "the sixth of the world". It had immense resources. Having made the revolution, how could the aim of building a socialist Russia be rejected? As Bukharin argued, then it would appear that the mensheviks had been right, the October revolution had been premature. The slogan appealed to the still-very-real enthusiasm of the activists, and touched a nationalist chord too: we in Russia are pioneers, we will show the world. Mayakovsky had imagined "Ivan leading the slum-dwellers of London out of their basements". The internationale might unite the human race, but Moscow will show the way. A heady mixture, skilfully used by Stalin against the opposition.

Naturally, Trotsky denounced Stalin's claim that by 1936, socialism had *already* been built, for such a claim rested on defining socialism as the (almost complete) elimination of capitalism and private enterprise. By 1936 virtually all industry, trade, construction and transport had been nationalized, agriculture was predominantly collectivized. The "Stalin constitution" was adopted. So this was socialism. Or was it?

2. THE NATURE OF STALINISM

Let us now take a look at the end of the thirties, when "Stalinism" had fully established itself as a political, social and economic system, leaving till later the task of identifying the changes which have occurred since. What relationship did the Stalinist system have to Marxism in any form? What was, or could be, a marxist explanation or justification for such a system? Its key features could briefly be identified as:

a) Despotic rule by reference to a supreme despot ("the cult of personality", to use Khrushchevian terminology).
b) A one-party state, but with the one party organized on centralized and strictly hierarchical lines.
c) Terror used, along with strict censorship, to enforce compliance with orders and with the formal ideology. Even suspicion of potential dissent was treated as a grave offence.
d) A highly centralized economy, run on hierarchical lines, with a minimal role for markets or other spontaneous processes, with top priority for investment in heavy industry, neglect of agriculture, consumer services, housing.
e) An emphasis, contrasting with the earlier period of bolshevik rule, on traditional virtues: patriotism, family, discipline at work and at school, conventional art forms, so-called "socialist realism" in literature, and so on.
f) Minimal rights for workers, no question of even partially free

trade unions, imposition of harsh delivery obligations on the peasants, after their forcible collectivization.

g) The Comintern reduced to a minor branch of the soviet foreign policy establishment, with large numbers of its officials shot in the terror-purges.

h) The emergence of a privileged stratum (class?) of office-holders in the state and party, the so-called *nomenklatura*, subject, however, to a high risk of arrest and worse.

Let us begin by examining the "Marxist" justification of the *one-party state.*

As already mentioned, there was nothing suggesting a one-party state in the works of pre-revolutionary Marxists. Indeed, the party is absent from Lenin's *State and Revolution.* But Lenin's views about his own party (not yet seen as the only one) caused deep suspicion in the mind of Trotsky. In a well-known criticism he made in 1904, he vigorously attacked what he called "substitutionism", i.e. substituting a centralized and authoritarian party for the working class in whose name it claimed to speak. "These methods (of Lenin) lead, as we shall see, to this: the party organization substitutes itself for the party, the central committee substitutes itself for the organization, and finally a dictator substitutes himself for the central committee" [31, p. 199].

Perhaps even better known is the view of Rosa Luxemburg. Opposing Lenin's conceptions and methods, she wrote in 1918: "Freedom only for the supporters of the government—however numerous they may be—is no freedom at all. Freedom is always and exclusively freedom for the one who thinks differently . . . With the repression of political life in the land as a whole, life in the Soviets must also become crippled . . . Life dies out in every public institution, becomes a mere semblance of life, in which only the bureaucracy remains as an active element. Public life gradually falls asleep. The few dozen party leaders of inexhaustible energy and boundless experience direct and rule . . . and an elite of the working class, is invited from time to time to meetings where they applaud the speeches of the leaders and approve resolutions unanimously . . ." [32, p. 134].

Was the suppression of all other parties a necessity of civil war? In part, yes. But the large majority of the mensheviks did their utmost to behave as a legal and loyal opposition, and Lenin's remarks on the subject are worth recalling. Referring to NEP, he said: "If a menshevik says: 'you are now retreating, I always was for retreat . . . , let us retreat together,' then we reply: 'for public expression of menshevism our revolutionary courts must shoot you, otherwise they are not our courts but God knows what" [30, p. 89]. Lenin was on record repeatedly at this period asserting the right and duty of the Bolsheviks to rule alone. The essential point was class analysis, and this of two kinds. The first was the (correct) view that, in a country overwhelmingly peasant, freedom to organize and to vote would inevitably mean that the peasant majority would threaten the Bolsheviks' hold on power and would mean the abandonment of what was seen as a long and hard road towards socialism. Democratic institutions, a genuinely elected legislature, were thus excluded, and this explains the attitude of the Bolsheviks to the Constituent Assembly and its large (peasant-elected) Socialist Revolutionary majority. The other is best expressed in the language used by Trotsky, the same Trotsky who had denounced Lenin's concept of the party:

"The special role of the communist party in conditions of proletarian revolution is quite clear. We speak of a class dictatorship. Within the class there are various strata, heretogenous attitudes, different levels of development. Yet the dictatorship of the proletariat requires unity of will . . .". Rejecting the notion of coalition with other socialist parties, he characterizes them as "representing various levels of backwardness and prejudices of the toiling masses". He continued: "We have often been accused that we have replaced the dictatorship of the Soviets by the dictatorship of the party. Yet we have every right to say that the dictatorship of the soviets became possible only through the dictatorship of the party . . . The communists express the basic interests of the working class . . . The dictatorship of the proletariat of its very nature implies the direct domination of the revolutionary vanguard . . . , which, where necessary, compels the laggard tail to catch up the head . . . [46, pp. 104, 105, 107].

Essential here is the axiom that *the* party represents by definition the interests of the proletariat and the views of its advanced-guard. Equally by definition, the view of any other party claiming to represent workers must be that of the "tail", laggards, backward, prejudiced elements, in due course labelled "petty-bourgeois" or worse.

Arguing at the Tenth party congress (1921) against the workers' opposition, Trotsky [46] declared that "they have placed the workers" right to elect representatives above the party. As if the party was not entitled to assert its dictatorship even if it temporarily clashed with the passing moods of workers' democracy . . . The dictatorship does not base itself at every given moment on the formal principles of workers' democracy". At the eleventh congress he repeated the same arguments: "The 'workers' opposition" puts forward dangerous slogans which fetishize the principles of democracy. Elections from within the working class, were put above the party, as if the party had no right to defend its dictatorship even when this dictatorship was temporarily at odds with (*stalkivalas'*) the passing feelings of workers' democracy . . . It is essential to have a sense of—so to speak—the revolutionary-historical primacy (*pervorodstvo*) of the party, which is obliged to hold on to its dictatorship, despite the temporary waverings of the masses . . . and even of the workers". Rejecting the workers' opposition demands for power to factory committees, he even more revealingly stated: "Formally speaking this is indeed the clearest line of workers' democracy. But we are against it. Why? For a basic reason: to preserve the party's dictatorship, and for subordinate reasons: management would be inefficient . . .". In these respects at least he was fully at one with Lenin. At the 13th party congress Trotsky's plea for inner-party democracy was necessarily muted by his own openly expressed fears that too much of it would leave room for alien elements to enter, and this is indeed an evident danger: if only one party is allowed, then views which would find expression outside might penetrate into it. He had no answer to Kamenev's retort: "If you say today, let us have democracy in the party, tomorrow they will say, let us have democracy in the trade unions, the day after tomorrow, non-party workers may well say: give us democracy too . . . , and then the millions of peasants . . ." [25, pp. 142–3].

Trotsky (and at that time Bukharin too) went further than most in demanding the militarization of the trade unions, but for Lenin there was no question but that the party must control them. This was in 1921, when Bolshevik popularity among the working class had much diminished. One more quotation from Trotsky may be apt in the present connection: "If it is true that compulsory labour is unproductive in all circumstances, as the Mensheviks assert, then all our construction-plans (*stroitel'stvo*) are doomed to failure . . . Without compulsory labour, without the right to give orders and demand their implementation, the trade unions would become a mere form without content, since the process of building a socialist society needs trade unions not for the struggle for better working conditions—that is the task of social and state organs as a whole—but to organise the working class for production, to educate, to discipline, to group, to attach (*prikreplyat'*) specific categories and individual workers to their posts; i.e. hand-in-hand with the government, to coerce (*vlastno vodit'*) the workers into the framework of a unified plan" [46, p. 136].

While Trotsky's "militarization" thesis was rejected, one can see in his formulation the essential elements of the Bolshevik attitude to free trade unions or indeed to any organizations, whether or not of the working class, that they do not control. In the Stalin period it was taken to be axiomatic that a party represents a class, and that, in a society without mutually hostile classes, there is room only for one party.

Stalin later provided a sort of justification for the intensification of coercion, asserting in a well-known passage that, on the way to its final withering away, the powers of the state have to be greatly increased, to deal with the resistance of the opposing classes. It is customary, in and out of the Soviet Union, to criticise Stalin for this formulation. Yet, again, an almost identical thought is to be found in Trotsky's works. In the process of criticising Menshevik arguments about the relationship between socialism and freedom, Trotsky asserted: "the road to socialism lies through the highest concentration of state-power (*gosudarstvennosti*). Like a light-bulb which, before extinguishing itself, flashes brightly, so the state, prior to its disappearance, takes the form of the dictatorship of the proletariat, i.e. of the most pitiless state, which coercively (*povelitel'no*) controls the life of citizens in all its aspects" [46, p. 161]. Over and over again, when he was "the prophet armed", Trotsky used arguments to justify extreme totalitarianism, and indeed also terror.

So one can say with some confidence that the Stalinist doctrines on the state and the party, in respect of their dominance over society in general and the workers in particular, rested on the firm foundations laid in Lenin's time, and reasserted by Trotsky and other Bolsheviks of the most varied hues.

Stalin added several elements. Under him the *centralized planned economy* was created on the ruins of NEP. (The "war-communism" episode of ultra-centralization was, in practice, what was described by Kritsman as "the most complete form of natural-anarchistic economy", anarchistic because there was no coherent central plan [21, p. 26]). While needless to say plans under Stalin were frequently contradictory and seldom fulfilled, none the less there was created an administrative planning-and-management hierarchy, which could impose central priorities on the economy and on society. This was part of the basis for his claim that "socialism" had triumphed in the USSR.

Stalin added the *terror,* and with it the systematic identification of any opposition, whether within or outside the party, with treason and interventionist plots. Not only could there be only one party, there could be no non-subversive opposition at all, even among its members. Hierarchy meant just that, and the principle of "democratic centralism" became totally meaningless (it was *becoming* meaningless soon after the revolution). Solzhenitsyn has argued that the "Gulag" was already fully formed under Lenin. Insofar as this related to repressive actions against what were seen as enemies of the revolution, this was so. But there was a vast quantitative and qualitative difference between the Cheka terror and the Stalin terror. During the civil war everyone's minds were concentrated on a temporary desperate emergency. Concentration camps, such as the notorious Solovki, did indeed become a feature of the Soviet scene after the civil war ended, and many a menshevik or SR found him or herself in *politizolatory* or exiled to Siberia. But this was action taken against political dissidents. Stalin's terror was distinguished by scale, by coverage and by motivation, and by brutality too. We still do not know exactly how many were arrested and detained in the 1930s, but certainly many millions. Among them were countless peasants ("kulaks", so-called, and others who opposed collectivization or stole from their "own" farms when they were hungry), and very large strata of Red Army officers, party secretaries, national cadres, intellectuals, party activists, and indeed very ordinary folk swept up in the great sweep of the purge. The motive was not any more one of isolating dissidents, or punishing specific actions; it was preventive, prophylactic, anticipatory. It spread to include families, subordinates, colleagues of those arrested. Charges, when made, were mostly fantastical, "proved" by forced confessions, but millions were sent to camps with no charge, simply by decision of an NKVD troika (the so-called *osoboye soveshchaniye*). All this was legitimated by reference to the theory that, as socialism is achieved, subversive resistance mounts and has to be pitilessly crushed.

To cite Vasili Grossman: "With Stalin's help the revolutionary categories of dictatorship, terror, the struggle against bourgeois freedoms, inherited from Lenin, and seeming to Lenin to be temporary, were made into the basis, the foundations, the essence, and merged with traditional, national, millenial Russian unfreedom. With Stalin's help these categories become the content of (Soviet) statehood, while survivals of social-democracy were turned into empty form, into stage decorations" [18, p. 189].

Stalin's concept of the party is perhaps best seen in his references to generals, officers, sergeants of the party. Hierarchy and obedience, uniforms with badges of rank, became part of the system with his active support. Similarly, Stalin strove to eliminate the traditional concern for egalitarianism, eliminating also Lenin's "party maximum", i.e. the rule that party members' incomes should be analogous to those of a skilled worker. In his speech against "petty-bourgeois egalitarianism" in 1931, he set the scene for the widening of the income gap between skilled and unskilled, bosses and workers, and the "Stakhanovist" campaigns then deliberately created a highly-paid group of record-breakers. Privileges of high officialdom were institutionalised, and increasingly (like Stalin himself) they separated themselves from ordinary people, living under guard in the Kremlin, special houses, dachas, etc.

Under Stalin the *nomenklatura* system was made fully operational. Its origins were in the first post-revolutionary years, when party members were assigned to key jobs throughout the republic. The secretariat, under Stalin since his appointment as general secretary in 1922, gradually made of this a system. Party dissidents were complaining about the appointments system in the early years of Soviet power, as many sources, and speeches at congresses, testify. This was an aspect of an essential feature of party control to this day, referred to in party resolutions as *podbor i rasstanovka kadrov* ("selection and placement of personnel"). This in practice meant selection replaced election in both party and soviet institutions. Provincial party secretaries, senior economic officials, editors, deputies to the "Supreme" Soviet, commanders of military districts, directors of research institutes, people's commissars (later renamed ministers), whosoever is supposed to elect or appoint them, became nominees to the appropriate section of the central committee apparatus. *Nomenklatura* meant both the list of posts which were subject to this nomination system and the list of persons deemed to hold such posts, who became known as *nomenklaturnye rabotniki.* (Note: a very common translation error is to render the work *rabotniki* as "workers", as in "*partiinye rabotniki*". Not to be confused with *rabochiye,* which really does mean "workers". In Soviet official language "rabotniki" almost always means "officials"). Inevitably this led to rank-consciousness, to a hierarchical structure to which appropriate levels of salary and non-monetary privileges were attached. With, it is true, especially under Stalin, a very considerable danger of sudden demotion, or worse.

The elimination of the "party maximum", referred to above, plus the compaign against "egalitarianism", meant that the privileges of high officialdom could not be publicly criticised, and the very existence of such privilege (and of special shops, dachas, seaside resorts) was made a state secret—which it remains to this day, along with any details of the *nomenklatura* system itself.

In an early work on the subject [38, p. 71], I likened the *nomenklatura* system to the *tabel' o rangakh* of Peter the Great. We will return to the theme of Stalinism as part of the Russian historical scene. At this point it is enough to note the similarity, a uni-hierarchy based on service, to monarch, state, party. Peter the Great as well as Stalin made the possession of rank and privilege full of occupational hazards.

We shall be examining various interpretations of the Stalinism phenomenon in subsequent pages. Here we will concentrate on Soviet interpretations of this period, and also of the post-Stalin stage of Soviet development. Unfortunately, the task is complicated by the silence which has descended upon any serious discussion of the nature and origins of Stalinism. Khrushchev's "destalinisation" campaign loosened many tongues, but his own explanation was sadly deficient: "the cult to personality", defects of Stalin's character, grave breaches of "socialist legality", causing many innocent victims among party members. But he insisted that Stalin's line had been correct until 1934, that is, that forcible collectivization, the excessive pace of industrialization, the centralized planning system, the political and social order created under the authority of the despot, were all correct. Needless to say, this was seen by many as highly unsatisfactory. Non-party victims of the terror were not referred to at all, and indeed nothing was done to "rehabilitate" the principal victims of the show-trials of the 1936–8 period: Trotsky, Bukharin, Rykov, Zinoviev, Kamenev, Rakovsky, remained either unpersons or enemies (though no longer with any mention of being agents of foreign powers). So, while under Stalin all oppositionists were branded as treasonable, under Khrushchev and his successors their ideas were at no point seriously discussed, any more than was the nature of the regime that had them killed.

Some analysts had recourse to Aesopian language and circumlocutions. Thus *Novyi Mir* published a review of a book on the fall of the Roman republic in which an intelligent reader could see an analysis of the rise of Stalin disguised as the rise of Augustus, with Trotsky cast in the role of Cicero ("killed in the 'forties, far from his native land, accused in the terminology of the time of being an enemy of the Roman people"). Another and longer article purported to discuss the rise of Mao, with virtually every word applicable to developments much nearer home. However, serious discussions inevitably were by word of mouth, or in *samizdat,* or in emigration.

It was there possible to raise *the* taboo question: how far was Stalinism the outcome of Leninism, or of Marxism–Leninism? Can its nature be discussed without decanonizing Lenin? *Samizdat* authors vary widely in these respects, ranging from Roy Medvedev's continuing attempts to stress the virtues of Lenin (and so the contrast between him and his bloodthirsty successor) to Solzhenitsyn's insistence that the evils of "Gulag" were already in full flower under Lenin. A full survey of these and many other ideas on this subject could fill a book, and would take us far from the subject. However, it may be worth citing the arguments of Vasili Grossman, the novelist, which are seldom cited in this content. In his fragmentary novel *Vsyo Techyot,* published abroad, he also helps to explain the massacre of the first generation of Bolsheviks, the "fanatics, destroyers of the old world", who genuinely believed and hated, who were "the dynamite with which the party destroyed the old Russia, clearing the space for new construction, for the granite of the idea of the great state". The first group that followed them, tough "builders" with minds of their own, also suffered heavily in the purges. "Terror and dictatorship swallowed its creators. The state, which seemed to be a means, became the end. Those who created this state thought it was a means of realizing their ideals. But it turned out that their yearnings and ideals were a means used by the great and terrible state. The state ceased to be a servant, became a grim autocrat. The state became master, became national in essence as well as in form, drove the socialist element into appearance, phraseology, a shell . . . ". Under Stalin, they needed not "servants, but civil servants". New men came forward to take the place of the fanatics and the first builders. Promoted young, they still occupied the top places in the hierarchy until today, they were the "Brezhnev" generation.

An odd characteristic of the Stalin period was an insistence on a uniquely wide gap between what was and what was claimed to be. To this Stalin himself made a direct contribution. Three examples can be cited. One was the "Stalin constitution", the "most democratic in the world", while a popular official song announced that "I know no country where man breathes so freely", this at the height of the terror. Another is Stalin's announcement, in 1948, that there were no slums in Moscow, at a time when overcrowding reached its highest point. Still another instance is his declaration, in 1933, that the people's living standards are rising, and that "whoever denies this is an enemy of Soviet power" (no wonder cost of living indices ceased to be published!). Sergei Utechin rightly observed that "Stalin's political theory was for the most part fictitious . . . There is little doubt that Stalin intended people to be aware of the fictitious nature of the theory, for an attempt on the part of the population to treat it as truthful (e.g. to believe that they enjoyed freedom of speech) would undermine the whole of his system of rule. Therefore any action based on belief (genuine or pretended) in the truthfulness of the official theory was treated as a most serious political offence. A profession of belief was obligatory, an action implying belief was severely punished [48, p. 242].

Perhaps today's official characterization of the Stalin era is implied by the definition of the more recent stage as that of "mature" or "developed" socialism, sometimes also called "real socialism" (not to be confused with Rudolf Bahro's *real existierender Sozialismus*). It emerged around 1970, apparently with Suslov's backing. It implies that the earlier period was one of immature or underdeveloped socialism. According to article by V. Dmitrenko [15] on the "origins of the conception of developed socialism", the transition to this stage was being completed "on the borders of the 'fifties and 'sixties". In his article, Dmitrenko refers to "the contradictions between the new potentials, the needs of social development, and old methods of control" (ibid., p. 8). This view finds many possibilities and ways of expression. If such terminology were not reminiscent of heresy (it had been used by Preobrazhensky, and Bukharin too), the earlier period could have been called one of "primitive socialist accumulation", characterized by the priority of accumulation, of vast investment projects, and also the preparation for and the waging of war. Economic historians and would-be reformers contrasted the "extensive" growth of that period with the needs of a more resource-constrained, efficient "intensive growth" that was now required. Economic calculation, consumer tastes, had been largely ignored, but could no longer be. In various ways, reforming economists would argue that the centralized system inherited from Stalin had become a hindrance to the development of the forces of production. The implication was that, when originally born fifty years ago, the system did fulfil its role, had its own rationality in relation to the tasks faced by the Stalin regime.

Dmitrenko, however, faced a difficult problem, that of reconciling the concept with the older notion of a transition period. "The experience of the USSR is ever more convincingly proving the need for a critical examination of the idea of a relatively short socialist phase and of the possibility after a transition period of the gradual establishment of consistently communist characteristics. The functioning real socialism showed the inadequacy of characterising it as a merely transitional society", which "bore the birth-marks of capitalism, such as commodity-money relations, the class structure of society, the existence of two kinds of property, the organic inequality arising out of distribution in relation to work, etc." [15, p. 6]. This, according to this author, led to unsound proposals to liquidate market relations, turn kolkhozy into state-farms, abolish producers' cooperatives, and "some of these proposals, unfortunately, were put into practice". The author deplores what he calls "the damaging consequences of overestimating the level of development of our society, of unrealistic approaches to the forms and tempos of the movement towards communism". This doubtless refers to Khrushchev's attempt to write into the revised party programme some specific promises about the transition to communism, such as free housing, free canteen meals, free urban transportation. These ideas have now been consigned to oblivion *sine die.* "Developed socialism" is here to stay for a long time, as a first stage, to be followed at some date by a higher stage of developed socialism, when "there will be created the conditions for a direct transition to communism" [15, p. 18]. This comes close to declaring "socialism" to be a mode of production, distinct from a shadowy communism of the future. This cannot be done in so many words, as it would be contrary to Marx's fundamental categories.

What is the significance of this sort of terminology? What does it tell us of regime's self-definition?

The Czech emigre Lubomir Sochor stresses the conservative functions of the ideology of "real socialism". "The affirmative function consists in justifying the established system at a time when it has lost its internal dynamism, in maintaining it in a state of immobility to make any change impossible, however necessary or urgent it may appear"; and "the negative (polemic) function . . . is so evident that there is no need to go into details. Its aim is on the one hand to repress, on the other hand to forestall. The ideology of 'real socialism' is the foundation of anathemas and maledictions decreed on schismatic ideologists . . .". It also "makes communist parties in power in the Soviet bloc countries immune against reformist ideas, if not once and for all then for a very long time. I am not suggesting, of course, that this ideology is the major cause of political and social sclerosis. On the contrary, it is determined by the latter and is merely its reflection and expression. But the ideology of 'real socialism' is an important factor in maintaining the immobility of Soviet society. This ideology helps to make immobility a chronic social disease, it generalises it by adding intellectual immobility to the immobility of social relations and institutions". [42, pp. 10, 12, 13].

This is a particularly clear way of stressing the inherent conservatism of the doctrine. Sochor indeed gives philosophical underpinnings to this interpretation: "the ideological formula on 'real socialism' was based on the identification of 'real' with 'existing' and the 'essence' with the 'existence'". Adapting Hegel's well-known phrase, "the Soviet ideologies have pushed the identification of the 'rational', the 'real' and the 'existing' to absurdity . . . Their identity is purely static, devoid of internal tension and consequently unproductive and sterile . . . It changes while always remaining the same, the pace of the changes within the immediate" [42, p. 10].

The official terminology is indeed being used for legitimation and apologetics for whatever happens to be, but Sochor may be overlooking its more "reformist" implications. There is a parallel here with another apparently apologetic "law", Stalin's so-called basic law of socialism: the maximum satisfaction of the evergrowing needs of the people on the basis of the highest technique. When used in this way by Stalin, it does indeed seem to imply that whatever exists is, by definition, providing the maximum possible satisfaction, etc. etc. But even Stalin found this identification of real and rational too much to swallow, since he also said that socialism provides the possibility of achieving maximum satisfaction (and of rational planning), but of course it is not necessarily realized in practice. This at once opens up the possibility of discussion about optimal planning and overcoming existing inefficiencies, and so the formula proved not to be a bar to reform discussions, after Stalin died (while he lived, he and he alone could point to any but the most trivial gaps between what is and what ought to be).

Similarly, "real", "mature", "developed" socialism can be said to require major institutional changes, because the existing institutions and planning system were created in a period now implicity characterised as immature, underdeveloped socialism, in just the way adopted by Dmitrenko (see quotation [15, p. 26]). The "leaked" memorandum by T. Zaslavskaya argues that "the system of production relations and the mechanism of economic management reflecting it lags behind the development of productive forces". In other words, while the official formula can be and is being used to strengthen conservatism and immobility, it can be and sometimes is used in a "reformist" way. For example, under "mature socialism" the working class is more mature, better educated, so forms of subordination appropriate to an earlier period are no longer appropriate today, this being another of Zaslavskaya's arguments. In fact one could easily assemble a quite long list of articles and books which use the "mature socialism" formula as a "reformist" battering-ram. Indeed Gorbachev spoke of "the need to create an economic mechanism which corresponds to the needs of developed socialism" (*Pravda,* 11 December 1984). Probably it is "real socialism" that should be regarded as the inherently conservative form of words. "Mature" and "developed" can serve either the conservative or the reformist cause, depending on who interprets these words, even if they were intended by their authors to legitimize immobility and the preservation of the social-political status quo.

3. THE 'LEFT' CRITIQUE

For many years now the Soviet experiment has been studied and criticised by Marxists of what might loosely be called a Trotskyist persuasion, i.e. by people who believe that the revolution was "betrayed", that it departed from true socialist principles. The same sort of analysis was aimed also at other countries that claimed to be socialist. Some temporarily embraced Maoism as an alternative, but the subsequent evolution of China has led to what could be called a generalized demaoization. For example, Coward and Ellis wrote the following: "In China another revolution in ideology is taking place, overthrowing ideas of delegation, management, the handing of power to 'representatives' or 'responsible individuals'; ideas which are the keystone of capitalist production relations and bourgeois democracy. They are being replaced with ideas of collective decision-making, of active thinking by all the people".[1] It is highly probable that the authors now wish to forget what they wrote in the middle 'seventies. But this issue of unreal or semi-utopian criteria must be borne in mind throughout the pages that follow. It is easy indeed to list the many ways in which Soviet social, political and economic arrangements fall short of, or contradict, the ideas expressed at various times by Marx and Lenin. But some of the

[1] Quoted from a critical review, in *Radical Philosophy* (Winter 1979, p. 8).

ideas could be seen as inherently unrealizable in practice. To take one example, to which we will have to return at length, it is no conceivable use criticising the existence of "bureaucracy" (e.g. in economic management) if one is advocating "marketless" state planning, since bureaucracy and hierarchy then become inescapable functional necessities. That is, unless the term "bureaucracy" is simply used as a pejorative phrase indicating the bad habits of officialdom, and no less a person than Trotsky himself regarded such a view as both un-Marxist and superficial [45, p. 91–2].

All analyses and explanations of the type about to be analyzed face one major problem: that of adapting the traditional marxist class-based analysis to circumstances radically different to those envisaged by Marx. Property relations, the acquisition and disposal of surpluses through exploitation which arises out of *ownership,* are categories of thought which cannot readily be applied to Soviet reality without considerable modification. Clearly, the rulers of the Soviet Union, howsoever one chooses to define or identify them, do not individually own the means of production. It could be argued that the same dilemma faced Marxist analysts of the Tsarist imperial past; was it useful to see Peter the Great's Russia in terms of a ruling *class,* and if so of what class? Pokrovsky's efforts to fit the tsarist autocracy into conventional Marxist categories caused him to attach to Peter the Great the not-very-convincing label of representative of "merchant capital". Others disagreed. Trotsky himself, arguing against Pokrovsky, wrote an eloquent article significantly entitled "On the historical peculiarities of Russia", which some who call themselves Trotskyists find it convenient to forget. Indeed Marx himself, in his last years, puzzled over the question of the applicability of his doctrines to Russia, as is clear from successive drafts of his reply to Vera Zasulich and correspondence with Mikhailovsky.[2] This is linked with another controversial question: the existence within the Marxist canon of the "Asiatic mode of production", a point to which we will return. Russia was not only geographically half in Europe and half in Asia. Russian Marxists found Marx's views embarrassing, and most of this correspondence remained unpublished until well after the revolution. Yet paradoxically Marx's own consciousness that Russia might find a road to

[2] For a valuable discussion of this point, with supporting evidence, see Shanin [41].

socialism different from that of developed capitalist countries could serve as an answer to those who (like the mensheviks) had argued that Russia had to await mature capitalism before moving towards socialism.

Trotsky himself defended almost to the end of his life the notion that the USSR was a "degenerated workers' state", or a workers' state with substantial bureaucratic deformation, though of course he denied Stalin's claim that socialism had already been built. In exile he vigorously criticised the notion of "socialism in one country". This criticism should be seen in context, including the context not only of the history of the 1920's but also Russian grammar. As Richard Day [14] pointed out, Trotsky did not at first challenge the Stalin-Bukharin claim that socialism could be built in Russia.[3] One reason related to the implications of his own earlier theories of "permanent revolution": it was, after all, he, even before Lenin, who had argued that after the seizure of power one would have to go forward beyond the bourgeois-democratic stage, even in a predominantly peasant country such as Russia. Another was the consciousness that, given that revolution in advanced countries had not broken out, denial to the possibility of building socialism would be seen as defeatist, an admission that the mensheviks had been right about the "premature" nature of the seizure of power in 1917 (this specific point was made by Bukharin in anti-Trotsky polemics). The "grammatical" point is that the word "build" is ambiguous, unless it is used in either its imperfective or perfective aspect: *stroit'* is the process of building, *postroit'* is the completed action. Trotsky would certainly deny the possibility of *postroit' sotsializm* in one country, but was surely favourable to "building" it. Indeed in his pamphlet *Chto takoye SSSR*..., published in 1936, he quotes with approval the view that it is nonsense to assume that socialism will triumph simultaneously in many countries; there will be some "isolated" socialist states for a time.

Highly relevant to the present issue was his view, and that of some of his supporters (notably Preobrazhensky) as to what constituted the stages of "building" socialism. It was equated in their minds with the extension of the ownership of, and powers

[3] In my view Day overstressed the relative importance of foreign trade in Trotsky's argument, but on this views can differ.

over, the means of production on the part of the "proletarian" state, the reduction of the role of market forces. On this last point Preobrazhensky was more rigidly dogmatic than Trotsky. He insisted on seeing the basic struggle as one between "primitive socialist accumulation" and "the law of value", i.e. the market. Trotsky [47], as a number of his works show us, saw more clearly the role the market must still play "throughout the transitional epoch", and he did criticise Stalin for going too far too fast in and after 1930 in industrialization and collectivization. But despite this, Trotsky was inclined to see state ownership of the means of production as an essential stage in the process of building socialism, and the fact that, by 1935, state and collective ownership had become predominant seemed to him an important victory along the road. The problem was that the state was not what it should have been, the means of production were controlled by a powerful bureaucracy acting in the name of the dictatorship of the proletariat. The bureaucrats did not *own* the means of production, they ruled in the name of the proletariat, so, even if the real proletariat had few rights, none the less in some essential way it was a workers' state, albeit a highly distorted one.

This was too much for some Trotskyists, and even Trotsky himself in the end found it increasingly difficult to call the terroristic despotism of the late 'thirties any kind of workers' state. Judicial forms are one thing, reality another. When he referred to the "bureaucracy . . . freeing itself from the market and from Soviet democracy", he at least showed some consciousness of the fact that market and democracy were not mutually inconsistent antitheses, that there were circumstances in which the greater power of the state machine over the economy actually reduced the influence of ordinary people (the workers too) over their lives and environment. There was no necessary coincidence between the expansion of state power and the building of socialism. One had at the very least to ask: what sort of state is it? Whatever illusions there may have been in Trotsky's mind in his first years of exile, surely no marxists can now seriously regard the Soviet state as a "workers' state" in any meaningful sense.

State capitalism is the label which some other "left" critics prefer. The term is not without its ambiguities, as when Lenin used it to designate a species of mixed economy in which real capitalists were still playing some economic role. In the present instance, the argument is that the state plays the role of capitalist. The state owns and controls the means of production, dominates society, appropriates and disposes of the surplus, allocates resources, with little or no control from below over its decisions. This could be regarded as a sort of ultimate development of monopoly-capitalism, with the state as monopolist, the state as exploiter.

One obvious problem with such a theory is to identify who are the "proto-capitalists", *who* do the exploiting, the deciding, the appropriating. The party leadership? High Officialdom? The bureaucracy? Those who control any means of production, everyone down to junior management? Another is to define what it is that they appropriate: the entire surplus, or that part of it which they use for their own privileged purposes? Or, to put it another way, are they exploiters because they have power of decision, or because of what they decide? Would a dominant group of ascetic monks who exercise a paternalistic dictatorship also "qualify" as exploiters, even if they were genuinely ascetic?

But let us return to the notion of the "collective capitalist", for it is clear that no individual, however high in the hierarchy, owns factories and farms. The collectivity of rulers *jointly control* the means of production and dispose of the surplus. They would then be seen as the equivalent of a ruling *class*. Let us put aside for the present the problem of identifying just who is senior enough to be considered a member of this collectivity. After all, similar imprecision inevitably attends the definition of "capitalists" in the real Western societies. Perhaps, though, one could question the validity or usefulness of the word "bureaucrat": apart from the authentic function of political leadership, what of (say) generals, organizers of vast projects such as the Baikal-Amur railway or north siberian gas, or for that matter the heads of the KGB? The word "bureaucracy" is associated with routine-bound office staffs. These do indeed exist in large numbers in the USSR, as elsewhere, but are they, or their normal *modus operandi,* quite what we have in mind in identifying the Soviet ruling stratum? Words like "elite" are not of much help either; some would stretch the vague term all the way to include a manager of a small rural store, on the grounds that he does command something, though his or her power is somewhat less than the manager of a branch of a retail chain store in Plymouth.

But let us turn to the usefulness of the term "capitalist". It is true that bureaucrats do carry out important functions which capitalists perform in capitalist countries. This has led some critics, for instance Charles Bettelheim, to insist that capitalism was not overthrown by the October revolution, that it exists still today [2]. This is linked with his definition of socialism, which includes control by the "direct producers", the elimination of commodity production and the wages system, and so on, and his belief that the term capitalism covers virtually every conceivable alternative to socialism so defined.

Yet to see the Soviet system as a variant of capitalism is surely to obscure some rather important differences. The point is well put in the Feher–Heller–Markus volume [16, pp. 23–25]: "in what sense can societies characterized by an absence of private property in the means of production, by the far-reaching reduction of market mechanism . . . by a dissolution of the institutional separation between economy and state and by a general tendency to abolish the distinction between the public-political sphere and that of civil society—in what sense can such societies be called capitalist at all?". Of course certain similar tendencies exist elsewhere, but "the difference between East and West is not one of degree". They also and very effectively argue that the treatment of these societies as *capitalist* must make them appear as quite irrational and inefficient, violating the "economic rationality" of any sort of capitalism. They have, they rightly insist, a rather different goal-function: not the search for higher profit, but what Feher *et al.* call "the maximization of material means (as use-value) under the global disposition of the apparatus of power as a whole" [16, p. 65]. Furthermore, the specific economic problems of soviet-type economies are radically different to those typical of capitalism, both in terms of the dominant criteria and in respect of outcome (generation of shortages, overcommitment of resources, the role of imposed plan targets, lack of feedback via the price mechanism, and so on). As one possible approach to an analysis of a complex phenomenon, "state capitalism" does help to clarify certain issues, but it confuses by implying a degree of similarity with really existing capitalism which is surely misleading.

The point was well put also by Castoriadis [9, p. 66]: "In seeking to define this economic formation, it becomes evident that it presents no analogies with the capitalist economy, since, despite the continued existence of exploitation and the monopolization of management of production by a social stratum, its economic laws are quite different". Arguing that the Soviet system has abandoned specifically socialist goals, he claims that it is "neither capitalist, nor socialist, nor on its way towards either of these forms", and that consequently "the Soviet economy represents a new historical type, and it matters little what one calls it so long as its fundamental basis is understood".

An alternative approach is that of a *transitional society*. This case can be presented in several variants, one of which resembles that of the "degenerated workers' state" referred to above. The defenders of the "transitional society" view would all agree that the Soviet system is some sort of amalgam or hybrid of elements of capitalism and socialism. There is public ownership of the means of production, but distribution rests on "bourgeois right". There is planning, though of a bureaucratic and undemocratic sort, commodity-money relations are reduced in scope, but they do play some role. A wages system still exists. Enterprises, provinces, ministries, compete for resources. The "associated producers" do not meaningfully control either the work process or the product. Thus it is not socialism. Neither is it capitalism.

Then what is it, dynamically interpreted? Is it evolving *towards* socialism? Or reverting back to capitalism? Or in a state of arrested development, in a sort of cul-de-sac? If it is a cul-de-sac, is it a durable and viable one, possibly even a mode of production not foreseen in the marxist tradition? The "transitionalists" have to reject the last of these possibilities, for their case rests on the belief that there is no lasting resting-place between capitalism and socialism. It has to be one or the other, or else one is either in movement in one or other direction or doomed to collapse in some unworkable hybrid state.

There are some useful insights to be gained by stressing the coexistence in the Soviet system of contradictory elements, and the attempt currently being made to reform the centralized planning structures highlights some of these contradictions. The limited power and ability of "the centre" to control its subordinates, or even to ensure coordination at the centre, the growing need to use the methods of commodity-money relations (the market) and the strong resistance of the party-state apparatus to such a development, problems of labour discipline and of linking incentives to the desired final result, these and similar problems are acute today. The plan supposedly incorporates use-values, i.e. the disaggregated needs of society (both of the citizens and of the productive units), but when "the only connection between consumption and production is realized through the administrative decision of a centralized and hierarchical bureaucracy" [16, p. 14] the outcome differs from both the intention of the planners and the requirements of the users. It might therefore be argued that the basic contradictions of the system arise out of its transitional and hybrid nature, and so the task is to find ways of overcoming the resistance of the ruling bureaucracy who have usurped workers' power and then move towards real socialism.

There are, however, some snags about this whole position. One of these relates to the definition of socialism which the advocates of this interpretation tend to adopt. For Mandel, or Bettelheim, or Ticktin, it broadly accords with Marx's socialism/communism, with planning as the democratic task of all the associated producers, with no market (commodity-production), no exchange, no bureaucracy, no money, no wages . . . If this conception is in fact an irrelevant and meaningless utopia, then obviously one cannot be in transition towards it. Without for a moment denying the many contradictions which the present system faces, the dynamic of possible changes cannot in fact be in the direction envisaged by the "transitionalists". Worse still, as they regard the market and socialism as inherently incompatible categories, they must view the market elements that exist as the "capitalist" part of the hybrid. This is another version of the error already referred to above, of regarding to extension of state power over resources and people as somehow synonymous with the "building of socialism" and victories in the class struggle. As if, for example, herding peasants into pseudo-collective farms represented an increase in the control of producers over their work or their product!

At present it means oppositions to "market" type reforms, in the name of non-existent and ill-definable "democratic" planning, with the unintended effect of supporting the most conservative elements in the bureaucratic power-structure. These, of course, resist reforms which reduce, or threaten, their grip on the economy. Trotsky's abovecited reference in the same sentence to "the market and Soviet democracy" is ignored or misunderstood. The "transitionalist" view in all its versions rests on what might be called a utopan alternative. To illustrate, let me cite an example. Suppose a productive unit exists, and requires for its activities ten material inputs. In the real world there are precisely two ways in which these can be acquired. One is by purchase, from their producers or via trading intermediaries. The other is by administrative allocation, requiring an allocational bureaucracy with appropriate powers (which involve social powers too). The bulk of the "transitionalists" counterpose to both these alternatives a mythical democratic planning process in which the ten inputs are somehow transmuted in the right quantities and at the right time by comradely discussion among the "associated producers". Faced with elementary questions about how this might work in practice, they seek refuge in one of two lines of defence: either they assume the achievement of "abundance", so that there will be enough for everyone, and mutually exclusive choices (and virtually all economic problems) will be a thing of the past; or, more commonly, one is treated to a diatribe in which the ill-effects and distortions attendant upon the market and competition will be listed. These, needless to say, are far from imaginary, and present authentic problems, economic, political and social. But how are they to be avoided? One last instance will suffice. In arguing against the present author, Ben Frankel (in *Radical Philosophy,* spring 1985) points out quite legitimately that if there is both central planning and market-type decentralization, some decisions taken at the lower (say at the enterprise) level will conflict with central plans. Surely, this could happen. But the only way of ensuring that they do not is to concentrate all decision-making at the centre, which is both undesirable and impossible.

Involved directly or indirectly in all these discussions is the issue of *class*. If a group of people, cven if not individual owners, even if unable to pass on their rights and powers to their children—actually control the means of production, are they a class in the marxist sense of that word? Some argue so, contrasting the juridical position (ownership by the "state" or "the people") with the real power relations. Castoriadis, in his already-cited work, argues that "bureaucratic property is neither individual nor collective", that is it "exploited jointly (*en commun*) by a class, collective within this class, in which there are still internal differentiations. In this sense it can be called "private collective property" [9, p. 85]. A similar case is put by Claude Lefort [29, pp. 147, 150]: "the political apparatus forged by the revolution, having eliminated the old dominant social strata, freed itself of all control on the part of the proletariat; this political apparatus then directly subordinates to itself the apparatus of production", and then is itself "pitilessly subordinated" to the task of management of the economy. Whence the existence of "a new hierarchy whose common denominator is that it directs, controls, organizes at all levels the production apparatus . . .". He too speaks of a "new class", collectively appropriating, and he interprets the Stalin terror as the way of disciplining this apparatus. Unlike the capitalists, whose power rests on the activities (and ownership) of individual capitalists, "the bureaucrats form a class (because) only their functions and status differentiate them collectively from the exploited classes". And, of course, Djilas had long ago written of the "new class" which controls, distributes, redistributes.

There is, however, some danger of seeing the stratum or class as "parasitic", a view also to be found in Trotsky, and which follows from his (surely superficial) analysis of the power of the "bureaucracy" in terms of its regulation of distribution. While of course some "bureaucrats" may be surplus to requirements, surely it is going too far to imagine that the economy and society can function with no political leadership, or that one can have plans without planners, economic ministries without offices, armies without staffs. This is part of the cost of using terms as "bureaucrats" with a pejorative implication, a fault already referred to.

In her interesting book, Maria Hirszowicz also identifies a "sovereign bureaucracy", but even high officialdom "must observe the rules imposed from above and follow the instructions of their superiors. A hierarchy—or rather a network of hierarchies—within the party state implies for this very reason the concept of 'more' or 'less' power, rather than a simple division between rulers and ruled" [22, p. 93]. This is not very different from David Lane's [28, p. 159] "competing elites in a bureaucratic structure", and he too would reject ruling class. But these two critiques are not from a "left" perspective, if by this is meant an attitude with direct or indirect links with Trotskyism or Maoism. There will be more on the relevance of the concept "class" in the final section. We should now turn to those who might be called neo-marxists, whose inspiration might be called revisionist, or who have in fact abandoned marxism after having earlier professed it.

Finally, it is worth recalling that virtually every possible interpretation of the system had already emerged in discussions among exiled oppositionists at the end of the 'twenties. We will have occasion later to cite Rakovsky, but here is Ciliga's 1936 account: "Some of us thought there was still a dictatorship of the proletariat, though it had a bureaucratic slant; others that there was no proletarian dictatorship left, but there were relics of it . . . Still others that there was no dictatorship of the proletariat at all and that we were faced with a new social regime that was neither bourgeois nor proletarian. Opinions on the Soviet economy were equally divergent. Socialist economy, transitional economy, typical bureaucratic economy, capitalist state economy" [12, pp. 124–5].

4. "EUROCOMMUNIST" AND OTHER NEO-MARXIST INTERPRETATIONS

Konrad and Szelenyi [26], two intelligent and imaginative Hungarians, argue for the notion of a ruling class of intellectuals. Their case rests in part on the undoubted fact that the days of unlettered commissars are over, that higher education is the path to power, that members of the ruling strata (class) must at least claim either professional competence or the knowledge of Marxism–Leninism (and thus the ability to read the compass of history), and preferably both, so their legitimation as individual holders of power-positions rests on an intellectual (or pseudo-intellectual) basis. This is supported in their analysis by the notion that the intellectuals as a whole live on the surplus generated by the productive workers, and this underlines the existence of a gap between intellectuals (or workers by brain) and proletarians (workers by hand).

It is true that there is a specific relationship between intellectuals and the regime, especially in some East European countries, notably Hungary. It is also true that some intellectuals do enjoy both power and privilege. However, one must, in the first place, be careful about how to define an intellectual. There are two opposite dangers. One is to adopt the old Russian notion of the *intelligentsia,* with its connotation of dissidence and creative critical thought. Obviously, *such* intellectuals cannot, almost by definition, be too near the seats of power. The other is to define intellectuals simply by possession of educational qualifications, in which case not only Brezhnev but an ex-Notre-Dame professional footballer are "intellectuals", and so (if he has a degree) is the Duke of Argyll.

Some privileged members of the upper *intelligentsia,* for example academicians, do indeed enjoy very considerable status and privilege, but should be seen more as very senior servants. Under Stalin, the "wrong" views even on strictly scientific matters could lead to disastrous personal consequences (for instance, for Vavilov), and in more tolerant times Sakharov finds himself in exile for interfering in politics.

Defining "intellectual" more reasonably as a person whose career and promotion are decisively influenced by intellectual qualifications of some sort, it is hard to avoid the very different conclusion of Bienkowski (a Polish ex-minister of education): "promotion in the ruling group . . . excludes all meritocratic criteria such as qualifications or talent. The ruling apparatus takes particular care that nobody that even once betrayed a critical attitude to any problem . . . should be promoted [3, p. 207]. A similar point is made in the emigre journal *Sintaksis*: intellectuals, again almost by definition, seek to assert their intellectual qualities in pursuing their careers, but promotion within the hierarchy does *not* proceed on the basis of ability, the key qualities being adaptability, conformism, loyalty to one's boss, so that, in the opinion of that author, intellectuals suffer much anguish and frustration [24, p. 57–77].

One can recall the ideas of Makhaisky (Machajski) at the beginning of the century: he saw Marxist social-democracy as the ideology of the intellectuals, using the workers and peasants to remove landlords and capitalists and to ensure the rule of the intellectuals. It could possibly be argued that the dominance of the revolutionary intelligentsia in the first years of the Bolshevik revolution lends support to Makhaisky's theories. But in the USSR the Marxist *intelligentsia* was dealt a shattering blow, most of them perishing in the Stalin terror. Their successors, for all their sometimes half-baked education in *rabfaki* and technical colleges, had other qualities.

Then one must not overlook the fact that the vast majority of the "beneficiaries" of higher education receive little pay and negligible privileges. Teachers, medical personnel, office staffs, librarians, activities classified as *Kultura,* even graduate engineers and technologists, earn on average less than skilled workers, and have (relatively) lost ground in the last twenty years in all communist-ruled countries. Many of these underpaid professions have become feminized in consequence.

Finally, it seems odd to regard the intellectuals as a whole as if they were exploiting the "direct producers" by living on the surplus they generate. It is surely a misapplication of the already very dubious distinction between the "direct producers" (defined narrowly as workers by hand) and the apparently unproductive "other ranks"; these latter would then include so heterogeneous a group as members of the politbureau, traffic police, technologists, industrial designers, philosophers, school janitors, nurses, economists, firemen, kindergarten teachers, party ideologists, novelists and shop assistants. Of course by no means all are intellectuals in any definition. The one thing they have in common is not being "direct producers" in the narrow sense used, surely wrongly, by Konrad and Szelenyi. It simply does not make sense, in any economy, whether socialist or capitalist, to regard all such persons as exploiters of productive labour.

The question of "who exploits whom" applies also, though in a different way, to the ideas of those of the Trotskyist persuasion who see an exploiting class in the USSR. We will have to return to this question yet again later.

Another school (or schools) interpret the Soviet system as having taken peculiar shape due to the backwardness of Russia, and this merges into the application to the Soviet Union of the notion of oriental despotism, or, in some versions, of feudalism.

Long before 1917 Plekhanov wrote: "A premature socialist revolution could lead to a political monster similar to the ancient Chinese and Peruvian empires, i.e. to a renewal of tsarist despotism with a communist lining". Many years later Wittfogel [49] wrote his challenging "Oriental despotism", which stressed the role of irrigation in the ancient empires, and this made its direct application to the USSR less than obvious. In the USSR itself this was virtually a banned subject under Stalin. Even in 1984 the attempt by one Yu.

Semyonov to discuss "Marx and the Asiatic mode of production" attracted criticism, though of an academic kind: Semyonov is said to have "sought to assert a hypothesis on the existence of a social order founded exclusively on the supremacy of state property, with a total co-incidence of the exploiting class with the state apparatus", which could be called "politarian" (*politarnyi*). This sort of formulation evidently raises sensitive issues, and the Soviet critic prefers to fit the ancient despotism into the category of a "slave society" with a large role for the state machine [37, p. 132].

We have already discussed "Russian backwardness" and Russian political culture in connection with the phenomenon of Stalinism. Neo-Marxist (and non-Marxist) critics in eastern and central Europe find obvious attraction in the idea that Soviet socialism was a backward and primitive sort. Many Eurocommunists, for instance in Italy, think likewise. This links with the position of most Mensheviks: the Bolshevik revolution was premature, the needed pre-conditions were lacking. As already noted, even the official doctrine of "mature" socialism implies an earlier stage of "immature" socialism. However, unlike the official doctrine, the neo-Marxist critics do not accept the notion of a "mature socialism" today. In their various ways, they assert or imply that the Russian legacy of social and economic underdevelopment, traditions of autocracy and serfdom, civil war and isolation in a hostile world, led to distortions both substantial and lasting. Having started, or been forced, onto the path of despotically imposed "revolution from above", they moved further away from the original doctrines and aims, and now exhibit features which repel many socialists, especially those who have absorbed Western humanist and democratic traditions.

Such critics vary widely in their approach. Some continue to regard Lenin as a basically positive figure, Stalin as having destroyed Lenin's legacy as well as most of his comrades. But an increasing number now ask themselves whether Lenin's one-party state, his intolerance of all opposition, his identification of the dictatorship of the proletariat with that of the party, his ban on factions within the party, made a major contribution to the features of the Soviet system they most dislike. Of course they are prepared to recognise that the pathological distortions of the period of the Stalin terror are past history. But the present regime is seen by them, and not without reason, as similar in essence to that of high Stalinism, minus mass terror and a demi-god despot, of course.

The Asiatic mode, or other societies where domination is quite evidently not based on an *owning* ruling class, have been used as a parallel by many brought up in the Marxist tradition. Bukharin [7, p. 69] made an early reference to the empire of the Incas, in which a non-property-owning priesthood dominated society, and Plekhanov has already been quoted. More recently the oriental despotism notion played a big role in Bahro's analysis of *real existierender Sozialismus,* and also in Alvin W. Gouldner's last works [17, p. 334]. There are problems in using this perhaps too imaginative parallel. The purely personal-despotic element relates above all to Stalin, and applies with much less force to his successors. Marx's "Asiatic mode" was static, based upon a predominantly rural society, and this fits badly into explanations of an industrializing and modernizing despotism, be it of the Peter the Great or a Bolshevik variety—though Gouldner argues that the inertia and lack of dynamism of today's USSR can be interpreted by reference (*inter alia*) to the "Asiatic mode", in which pressure from above is the only way to overcome the system's tendency towards inertia.

So, while some feature of the Soviet system do recall elements related to what loosely can be called oriental despotism, possibly a better approach treats them as pre-capitalist, a return to a species of neo-feudalism. Markus [16], in the volume cited above, speaks of "relations of dependence" (*Herrschaft und Knechtschaftverhältnisse,* i.e. of domination and subjection). It is no coincidence that a bold Soviet theorist, Danilova, asserted that the economic factor played a decisive role under capitalism, but that in both *pre*-and *post*-capitalist society the key factor was that of domination-subjection [13, p. 48].

Again, there are some elements in the system that may merit the designation semi-feudal. Markus [16, pp. 38–9] refers to "striking remnants of some traditional social organization", including "the use of forced labour . . . elements of semi-bondage to land . . . , the role of non-monetarised covert privileges in the upper strata of the social hierarchy", as well as "degrading personal dependencies". Bienkowski [3] among others, also speaks of a "process of feudalization", Voslensky [50] of "feudal fiefs". The use of such a term is questionable, in that in classical feudalism the lords exercised personal power (with fortified castles and even private armies), in contrast with a Soviet high official (or even a tsarist *dvoryanin*), whose power derives solely from position, from rank.

The image of feudal or oriental-despotic relations has its uses, highlights certain specific features of Soviet-type systems. It is not for nothing that Bukharin referred to Stalin's policy as the "military-feudal exploitation of the peasantry". The more one stresses the specifically Russian features of Bolshevism, the more likely are such images to appeal, the more so as the Russian revolution was in part a revolt against (capitalist) modernization, a rejection of the "European" and indirectly the reassertion of older and cruder ways of ruling and industrializing. However, the Soviet system cannot, in my view, usefully be seen as inherently feudal or "Asiatic", even if some features of the system have undoubtedly some resemblances to older modes and traditions. If Szelenyi, Castoriadis, Markus, are right, and this is a new hitherto unknown social formation, its peculiarities would be obscured by too much use of labels which relate to very different societies and historical periods. The extension of this system (with varying degrees of success, admittedly) to countries with quite different traditions is used by Markus and his colleagues as a further refutation of the "oriental-despotic" type of interpretation, but this is not too strong an argument: such countries as East Germany, Czechoslovakia and Poland would scarcely have adopted this species of system without external coercion, whereas in the USSR it grew for reasons internal to that country, organically.

Many critics, who may differ in other respects, see the close connection between political and economic power, the vital link between centralized planning and the centralized party-state machine, between privilege and the function of managing and allocating, the essentially hierarchical nature of economic (market-less) administration and the hierarchical organization of power and of society. Thus Selucky [43], Dora Shturman [44], and also Feher, Heller and Markus [16], stress the effect of the lack of economic and institutional feedback, the weakness of the citizen as a consumer and as a claimant on resources. The title *Dictatorship over Needs* speaks for itself. The powers-that-be do not, of course, simply ignore the needs of society, indeed they adopt a paternalistic posture. The point is that it is for them to decide, they know which are the needs that should be satisfied. Control, the combatting of spontaneity in any sphere, become aims in themselves, and much will be said in the next section about the resultant contradictions with an increasingly necessary stress on economic rationality.

Finally, there is among some non-Marxists (some neo-Marxists, too) a debate about the meaning and appositeness of the word "totalitarian" in relation to the Soviet system. Its use may be justified by the following consideration. There are three basic species of power: political (and police), economic, and ideological-religious. In Western societies they are in separate hands, even if there are some links between them, and this provides considerable freedom of manoeuvre for any adroit citizen, as does the disunity (in a democracy) of various segments of political-and-police power, e.g. a multi-party system, some degree of separation between legislative, executive and judicial authorities, federalism, and so on. In the Soviet system in principle all these powers are in the same set of hands. This, plus the degree of control over the press and other media, and the tendency to repress any unofficial association or pressure group, justifies the use of the label "totalitarian". The Soviet ideologists' own indignant opposition to the very notion of "pluralism" points in the same direction. Confusion has (in my view) arisen because of a misunderstanding over the possible meaning of the word "totalitarian". If it is taken to mean real total control, a pure hierarchy in which subordinates have no influence over decision-making and always obey orders, with no pressure groups existing at all, then of course the Soviet system is not totalitarian. Sectional interests do find means of expression within the nominally monolithic party-dominated structure, orders are frequently drafted by their recipients, not all orders can be or are obeyed. Because plans are frequently contradictory, ambiguous, unfulfillable or unfulfilled, some scholars deny that the Soviet Union's economy is planned. This would be a correct judgment if one defines "planning" to require a set of coherent, clear, fulfillable, balanced plan-orders.

So "totalitarian" is a useful label. Others have devised alternatives: "Partocracy" (Avtorkhanov [1]), "etatism" (Brus [4]), bureaucratic Leviathan" (Hirszowicz), "unihierarchy" (Rigby), "organic Labour State" (Harding [19]). As Shakespeare has said somewhere, "What's in a name?". A more important question is: what is the nature of the Soviet regime today? I would strongly agree with Feher [16, p. 8] and his collaborators when they wrote: "... A confrontation with the reality of these societies demonstrates deep conceptual ambiguities and inadequacies in the theoretical heritage of classical Marxism ..., and that these systems represent a social formation the possibility (and the danger) of which was not only unforeseen by Marxist theory, but in a sense could not have been predicted by it".

Very well, *what* social formation?

5. CONCLUSION: AN ATTEMPT AT AN INTERPRETATION

Having devoted many of the preceding pages to expounding and criticising the ideas of others, it now becomes necessary for the author to expose himself to others' criticism by attempting his own interpretation. This is not a strictly "Marxist" one, since I do not believe in "-isms" in general, Marx*ism* in particular; Marx's favourite quotation, "*de omnibus dubitandum*", can and should be applied freely to Marx himself.

The USSR does seem to be a genuinely new kind of social formation, or mode of production, unforeseen by Marx. Attempts to use conventional labels derived from (or applied to) something very different are bound to give a misleading impression, they have to be modified to fit the new sort of social and economic structure. In my own first attempts to grapple with these problems I was attracted to the notion of the universal service state, and so to Peter the Great. Suppose, I reasoned, there existed a society in which everyone held civil and military ranks: this rank-based and rank-conscious society would not be one to which the Marxist term "class" could be applied, since position and not ownership were the determining and defining factors. In Western society too we have senior officials and generals, but this can be held to be no more than a modification of (and to be understood in relation to) the basic distinction between those who own and those who do not. But suppose no one owned the means of production, and society was strictly hierarchical. The definitional problem would be where to draw the line, a necessarily rather arbitrary procedure. All officers, and their civilian equivalents? Senior officers only?

Of course no country can exist in which *only* rank determines position and influence: for example a widely-read author or great musician, or pop star, need hold no rank, and a successful black marketeer can make more money than a quite senior party secretary (unless he too becomes corrupt). In no country do orders simply travel downwards, without those "below" having some influence on their contents. It is also true that within any hierarchy everyone below the topmost level has to obey his (or more rarely her) superiors. Nor do even the "other ranks" of society merely passively obey; they may at times disobey or obstruct. None the less, though reality will always be more untidy than any model, the universal service state, or unihierarchy, is a useful way of looking at the essence of the system.

One hierarchy? Some might disagree. There are many, and they may be competing. This is partly true. There are hierarchies in the Soviet republics and regions, in management, in academe, in the central party machine, in retail distribution, the army, and so forth. Most people rise within their particular sphere or area. However, this would also be true in (for example) the British army. Thus a colonel in the Royal Corps of Signals will not be appointed to command an armoured division, nor does an infantry major expect to be transferred to command an artillery regiment. None the less, the army as a whole is a highly rank-conscious hierarchy, within which there are specialized sub-hierarchies.

What binds them all together is the appointment system. In the British army it is (or was, when I was a soldier) the Adjutant-general's department. In the Soviet communist party it is the party apparatus, who operate the *nomenklatura* system, under which the head of the trade unions could be transferred to the job of deputy foreign-minister and thence to the deputy-chairmanship of the presidium of the Supreme Soviet, to take the actual case of V. Kuznetsov. As the example shows, there is some cross-posting between hierarchies, though onc gathers that at lower levels one tends to rise within one's own particular locality or sphere (but this is also the normal pattern in the British army, up to the rank of major).

As all appointments to all posts considered to be significant (in political, social, cultural or economic spheres) are on the *nomenklatura* of the central committee, this seems a good definition to adopt, because it is a *self*-definition of the ruling stratum or class. As already pointed out earlier, I was struck in one of my first articles on the subject by the parallel with the tsarist *dvoryanstvo* (service-gentry) estate. Voslensky's book (*nomenklatura* [50]) specifically identifies this group with "the dominant class", "the directing class", "the exploiting class". It could be said, in answer to possible objections, that membership of the *nomenklatura* is not the *cause* but the *effect* of being in the ruling group. One is not a party secretary or general because one is in the *nomenklatura,* one is on the *nomenklatura* because holding these high positions so defines you within the system.

Privileges depend on rank and are lost when rank is lost, which may be one reason why there is such a pronounced tendency towards a geriatric leadership in the USSR—despite fairly generous "personal pensions". Rank is not, as such, hereditary. However, especially since Stalin's death, sons (much more rarely daughters) of senior officials benefit from sufficient educational privilege and other kinds of "pull" to achieve fairly senior positions in some sphere, for example in prestigious research institutes. To make the parallel with the tsarist system again, *dvoryanstvo* status was (with some exceptions) inherited, but could also be acquired by promotion in the civil and military service, while some hereditary *dvoryane* held minor jobs (or small areas of land), and some—notably Lenin himself—even turned into professional revolutionaries. It may well be that, if we had family histories of the *nomenklatura,* there would be evidence of similar downward mobility, but quite possibly less of it. But we lack the necessary evidence, and in any case even the *nomenklatura* lists (what appointments figure in it, how many are involved at various levels, and so on) are state secrets.

Inevitably, as society has become more stable and economic growth has slowed, social mobility has become less, and so a gradual tendency exists for the consolidation of a "class of rulers", who will tend to inter-marry and to make promotion from below more difficult to achieve. But surely they will never be stupid enough to close the door to advancement. Indeed, were it otherwise we would be justified in referring to a *caste.* The old Russian word *sosloviye* (estate, a rulers' estate) may be suitable because it is unfamiliar, and yet reminds us (perhaps too much?) of parallels with the past. Still another approach emerged in the debate between oppositionists in Russia itself, before they were liquidated. Rakovsky [40], could see that most of the men around Stalin were *former* workers, that they turned into full-time *agenty vlasti* (agents of authority), and in doing so ceased to be workers. This is obviously true, and represents a belated realization of the inherent meaninglessness of the "dictatorship of the proletariat". He might have gone further, and noted the fact that, in most societies, persons promoted from below value their privileges and pay little attention to the welfare of those who have now become their inferiors; to this the typical behaviour-pattern of sergeant-majors in any army bears eloquent witness. It helps to explain the *style* of the new men who rose with Stalin. In the course of discussion some anonymous oppositionists wrote [51]: "Before our very eyes there has been and is being formed a large *class of rulers* (*klass pravyashchikh*)". They then discussed whether they exercise state power as a species of private property. But the point in the present context is the words "class of rulers", as contrasted with the traditional Marxist "ruling class". This is more than a slight verbal rearrangement: if it is a class, it is so because it rules, whereas the Marxist would or should argue that capitalists rule (directly or indirectly) because of their class position as owners. Another example of the importance sometimes attaching to verbal reformulation is Bernard Chavance's [10] distinction between *capitalisme d'état* and *capitalisme étatique*; in the first version the *state* is the "capitalist", in the second the role of capitalists is played by "concrete persons" under the formal ownership of the state. I do not myself share the view that Soviet society is usefully designated as capitalist, and only cite this argument to illustrate the importance that can attach to verbal variations.

Clearly, anyone even remotely influenced by the Marxist view of history or society is bound to seek the sources of the power of the rulers (be they a class, stratum or estate) in their relationship to the means of production. The connection here leaps to the eye. They do collectively decide what to produce, how incomes are to be distributed, what the surplus should be used for, how much should be invested and in what. Many if not most of the rulers are economic controllers or managers, the economy is under the supreme command of the apex of the political hierarchy, the politbureau being in a real sense the board of directors of the biggest firm in the world, USSR Inc. As already argued above, it is no answer to retort that the power of the rulers is limited, that they are influenced, and sometimes disobeyed, by those below them. All power everywhere is subject to constraints of some kind, outside of bad textbooks on politics.

But which way round does power go? Can one meaningfully speak of political power being derived from the economic? Surely not. The two are intimately linked, they reinforce each other, but the dominance of the political is hardly to be doubted. The "class" interest is not profits, most certainly not economic rationality as such. Indeed, one of the biggest problems facing Soviet society today arises out of the resistance of the "class of rulers" to the sort of reforms which are required for a more rational operation of the economy; a contradiction exists between the interests of the system's rulers in maintaining intact their domination over the everyday operation of the economy and these rulers' interest in achieving the economic objectives of their own policies, which do require increased efficiency.

In 1921, Chayanov [11, p. 59] with remarkable prescience, wrote the following: "The system of communism put all participants in economic life into a system of standardized rewards (*voznagrazhdeniye*) and thereby deprived work of any stimulus. Of course, work was done, but effort was lacking, as it had no basis. The lack of stimulus affected not only the executants but also the organizers of production, since they, like officials (*chinovniki*) everywhere, were interested in the perfection of the act of decision itself, in the precision and polish of the work of the economic apparatus, and not at all in the results of its work. For them the impression created was more important than material results". He imagined a peasant utopia (in 1984!) in which such problems had been overcome. Markus [33, p. 245] made the point that "the goal-function of the 'planned' economic activities of the state" is "the maximisation of the material means (as use values) under the global disposition of the apparatus of power as a unified whole". He added: "What is effectively accumulated outside the domain over which it can directly dispense does not count (for the power apparatus) as part of the 'national' wealth, but constitutes a threat . . . because it can confer a degree of economic independence upon those who own it formally or practically". This is not unlike the observation of Ken Jowitt [23, p. 275]: "The Soviet elite may be expected to disdain as well as fear a social order based upon the skills and ethos of businessmen and (competitive) politicians and to avoid the benefits and terms of private/market ownership: they are too threatening.

But, to repeat, it is *also* true that, in their capacity as managers of USSR Inc., the rulers require that the economic system should function; one needs to be both "red *and* expert". In a conflict between power and efficiency one cannot give sole attention to power, if only because too much inefficiency causes loss of power, internally and externally.

What is the role, in this system, of Marxist ideology? This would be the subject of a book-length discussion. Some assert that ideology is dead, that it is either a formal catechism recited on appropriate occasions, or a card-index of quotations to justify a policy decided on practical grounds. It has important functions of legitimation, it is linked with important festivals and myths, is a new kind of "opium for the people". Any parts of the sayings of the founding fathers which happens to be inconvenient are forgotten or reinterpreted. It has been said, surely with good reason, that no member of the politbureau has the slightest interest in what Marx actually said on any subject.

Some (usually anti-Soviet) commentators claim that the regime is guided by ideology, *real* ideology. This, in their eyes, includes such characteristics of the system as the one-party state, censorship, ban on free trade unions, collectivized agriculture, militarism, capital punishment, privilege, hierarchy. Whatever the merits or otherwise of such a characterization of essential features of the system as it is today, this sort of approach *deduces* the ideology from what exists, and then asserts that ideology determines it—a not-very-useful tautology.

Yet ideology does influence policy and attitudes. There is, among the leadership, concern that policies should aim at improvements in living standards and welfare services, in line with a basically paternalist image. "Workers" are not just given pride of place in official speeches. Security of employment is a valued right, and workers have indeed, as we have noted, overtaken most "intellectuals" in the earnings league. Private trade is seen as immoral, as "speculation", not only because it is outside the power of the apparatus, and this negative attitude is widespread also among ordinary people (this is an additional obstacle to "market" type reforms today). Since in no country is any decision ever taken on *purely* ideological grounds, there is no way of measuring its impact, in either domestic or foreign policy. It can be seen either in terms of a "coloured-spectacles" image, or as blinkers, either colouring the way reality is perceived or excluding from sight some solutions to practical problems which might otherwise be perceived.

Does Soviet experience conflict with the basic tenets of the doctrine of historical materialism? Surely it does, on even the loosest definition of that term. To say, with Lenin, that "politics is concentrated economics" is not to escape from having to recognise the dominance of politics, the use of political (and police) power to change fundamentally the relations of production, to transform the economy and the working lives of millions of citizens. Economics, needless to say, is always present as a modifying and constraining factor, interacting with the political. But the latter has been dominant even "in the last analysis". This should in no way downgrade the importance of economic factors in the process of political decision-making. They do have a life of their own, as do also scientific-technical factors. One can no more legislate economic laws than order water to run uphill. But one can still arrest unofficial traders as speculators (and build dams to prevent water from finding its own level).

So far, the international aspect of "really existing socialism" has been ignored. Some Trotskyists ascribe much or even most of the distortions they see in Soviet development to the consequences of the "socialism-in-one-country" doctrine. If by this is meant the consequences of the espousal of the doctrine, this does not make too much sense, since the USSR's isolation was not a conscious aim of policy; it was a fact it was necessary to live with. If, however, the point is that the isolation of an underdeveloped Russia in a hostile world had a profound influence on events, policies and institutions, this was indeed the case. It is also true that, in Stalin's time and since, the great-power interests of the Soviet Union were given priority, or were explicity identified with the interests of the world communist movement. The questions that many ask, from left-wing or right-wing positions, are: How far is the USSR different from other great powers, how far does her professed ideology influence foreign policy, is it true that "world domination" is the goal of this policy, and, if so, what impels the Soviet leadership to adopt such aims?

A case can be made for a totally non-ideological interpretation. Let us, for example, look at the discussions between Molotov, Hitler and von Ribbentrop in 1940, fully documented in the German archives. The crudest considerations of great-power spheres-of-influence seemed to prevail. The occupation of the three Baltic states at this same period may have been accompanied by ideologically-orthodox declarations, but the objective as such would have been very well understood by any Tsarist minister. When war with Finland broke out in 1939, Stalin set up a "workers and peasants government" at Terijoki, under Kuusinen, and then, when its phoneyness was all too apparent, expunged its very existence from the record. (I fail to find any reference to it in Soviet histories of the period, or in Kuusinen's biography). Dominance over Poland and the Balkans was an aim of Tsarist policies. Methods have changed, it is true. Catherine II could get one of her lovers "elected" to the Polish throne, a solution unavailable to the present generation of Russian leaders.

Voslensky, in his book on *Nomenklatura* [50], develops the thesis that territorial expansion is, for Soviet officialdom, an aim which parallels capitalists' attempts to maximise profits. This seems to me far-fetched. So, in its own way, is Richard Pipes's double-edged thesis: that the Soviet system is expansionist and aggressive because of its essence, *and* that it was equally so in the case of the Tsarist empire, even though presumably it had a quite different essence.

The expansion of communism as such is surely not desired unless it is of the "moscovite" variety, as can be seen from the conflict with China (and, earlier, with Yugoslavia). The Soviets' evident desire for recognition as a super-power, with the right to nuclear parity and to have a say in the world's problems, requires no Marxist-Leninist doctrine to explain it. The United States prefers *pax americana,* and uses whatever weapons (military, ideological, economic) are to hand in defence of its position. The USSR's claim to parity, with the "capitalist" powers remaining dominant in much of the world, is consistent with an expansionist push, modified both by fears of unleashing a nuclear holocaust and by the limits set by the aim of maintaining Moscow's control; thus a good reason for not incorporating all of Germany in the Soviet empire (even if this were in other respects practicable) is the likelihood that in a Russo-German partnership it would not be long before the Germans were in charge.

To identify and weigh the relative importance of "normal" great-power objectives, of "Soviet" or Russian nationalism, and of residual ideological conviction, is probably impossible. It may well be that members of the politbureau are themselves unaware in what proportions they are motivated by these various considerations. Marx, as is almost universally admitted even by orthodox Marxists, significantly underestimated the importance of nationalism ("the workers have no fatherland"). We now know that no stratum of society is exempt from nationalist or racist feelings, and, precisely because the present leadership cadres have risen from among ordinary people, it would be astonishing if their views (also about women, modern art and much else) did not reflect the attitudes and prejudices of their *milieu.* No observer of the Soviet scene today can fail to note the importance of Russian nationalism as a "cement" for the regime. But of course too much stress on the *Russian* aspect is fraught with danger in a multi-national state, and so its extreme manifestations are repressed, a cult of *Soviet* patriotism advocated, but with Russians still presented as *primus inter pares,* an elder brother. It remains a matter of controversy among Western specialists how strong the non-Russian nationalisms are, how far they are likely to threaten the unity of the system. My own (doubtless fallible) judgment is that there is a tendency to exaggerate the centrifugal elements, that the republican hierarchies provide avenues of promotion for ambitious people of the main nationalities (the Jews being something of a special case). See Mary McAuley [36], who criticises the contrary views of H. Carrère d'Encausse and others. This is not to deny the existence of Ukrainian or Georgian nationalism, and of virtually open resentments in Estonia and Lithuania. But (as was the case also under the Tsars) this is unlikely to threaten political stability unless the regime is seriously weakened for other reasons. Much more serious is the resentment of Soviet domination in several East European countries, Poland especially, and it helps little that acceptance of Soviet policies is labelled as "proletarian internationalism". But it is not part of the present paper to indulge in prophecy.

How do the bulk of the population view the Soviet regime? Opinions vary, from Solzhenitsyn's picture of the people groaning under the tyranny of a tiny ruling group, to Alexander Zinoviev's view that the regime is accepted and more or less corresponds to popular desires. With regret one must conclude that—though he takes his argument too far—Zinoviev is nearer the truth. People do grumble, have many grievances no doubt, but hope to find remedies within the system, see no possibility to challenge it, and, more important, would probably oppose most proposals to reform it. Thus they do not like the shortage of meat, but would deeply resent the price increase which alone can get supply and demand into some sort of balance. There is no reason to suppose that the masses actually want socialism in a definition which would appeal to the radical *intelligentsia.* To cite Mihajlo Markovic [35, p. 312]: "But Marx did not solve the problem: how will the whole proletariat form its common will, make the step from a 'class in itself' to a 'class for itself', win power and run society 'organized as a ruling class'? How will this alienated and degraded class build up a consciousness about essentially new possibilities, a consciousness that requires enormous general culture . . . And if a vanguard of the class does the job, how to avoid the alienation of the vanguard, manipulation of the class by it?".

This brings us finally back to appropriate and inappropriate criteria. The Soviet system cannot usefully be judged or criticised in terms of an inherently unrealisable utopia. Having overthrown Tsars, landlords, capitalists, and later having destroyed the intellectual fanatics who flourished in the revolutionary years, an industrializing despotism imposed order, and in the name of a revolutionary ideology a "class of rulers" has become firmly established. It survived the death of the despot, shed the extremes of terror and personality cult, made life reasonably secure for all who do not wish to profess dissent. It is, after all, thirty years since anyone was executed for an overtly political reason in the USSR, a remarkable contrast to the preceding thirty years.

Yet the regime's search for stability is in danger of achieving immobility and decay, not least because the centralized system of economic-and-political management is increasingly in conflict with the development of the productive forces. It matters greatly, both ideologically and politically, to believe that "socialism" in its Soviet version can, in the foreseeable future, catch up and overtake the developed West. Khrushchev believed that it could. Experience has shown that this was not so, and this despite serious economic difficulties within Western capitalism. Analysts such as Bienkowski and Gouldner speak of "petrification", "stagnation", "inertia". The present leadership are aware of the challenge posed by the necessity of fundamental change. Their residual Marxist beliefs must lead them to be deeply concerned when quite visibly the relations of production act as a brake on the forces of production. We will soon discover whether they (or their immediate successors) can rise to the challenge, and what kind of new social forms (or conflicts) will be the consequence of the attempt. But at the same time the "residual Marxism" in their minds, as well as the self-interest and habits of most members of the ruling stratum, incline them to oppose the market-type solution, which, by whatever name is given it, seems to them both alien and threatening.

Brus [4,5] among others, has discussed with skill the relationship between democratization, market and efficiency. The experience of Hungary, and now also of China, suggests that while in some sectors at least (notably agriculture) the last two are closely connected, the first—democratisation—is much less so. The market, by giving more choice to consumers and producers alike, and thereby diminishing the everyday impact of "dictatorship over needs", does provide for an increase in economic freedom. It could even be said that this is a necessary condition, both for the introduction of any meaningful sort of workers' participation or self-management, and for the extension of democracy into the political-social sphere. Necessary maybe, but, in my view (and also Brus's) emphatically not sufficient. Not only Hungary and China, but also Chile and several other right-wing repressive dictatorships, demonstrate this all too fully. Still, what other path forward is there in Eastern Europe? The ultra-left can only counterpose a set of slogans about democratic planning without a market, which are recognised now even by most Marxists as being meaningless in practice.

This article has concentrated almost exclusively on the Soviet

Union, as a sort of prototype of "really existing socialism". However, the term itself was coined by Rudolf Bahro in his book under that title, and he was writing in East Germany, using the term in a quasi-satirical, critical spirit. It is therefore appropriate to ask what light the experience of other countries sheds on the subject of the present inquiry.

While their experience is important and relevant to any full analysis of the impact in practice of Marxist ideas in the world, including the possibilities of alternative ways of managing the economy, their virtual omission is not as serious a defect as might appear. Firstly, because in many instances (especially in Eastern Europe) the Soviet-type system was imposed by outside forces, so that many problems arose out of the conflict between the political culture (and economic interests) of the country concerned and the Soviet model which they adopted, or were forced to adopt. Secondly, the less developed "socialist" countries (Cuba, Vietnam, Mongolia, to some extent even China) are mainly of interest as models of economic development and modernization; it is in the USSR that the "mature" version can be studied. China may be, indeed is now, taking a new road. However, in their first years China's rulers followed the Soviet example fairly closely, and the dramatic departures from the Soviet pattern—the Great Leap Forward, the communes, and then the cultural revolution—are now interpreted in China itself as disastrous. (There are some historical parallels with earlier stages of Soviet development, however, which will not be pursued here). Time will tell whether the wave of market-type reforms, and the virtual decollectivization of agriculture, will eventually bring China to some new model of socialism, or whether this will prove a sort of delayed Chinese NEP, justified by the general poverty and low level of development.

There is much to be learned, and studied, in the experience of Hungary's "1956" and of the Hungarian "new economic model", in the advantages, obstacles, stresses, which accompany the attempt to introduce the market mechanism, to change Soviet-style centralized directive planning. The same holds for Yugoslavia's "self management" experience, though in the most recent years the Yugoslav economy (and the Hungarian too, though to a lesser extent) has encountered serious difficulties. Czechoslovakia's search for a new model ("socialism with a human face" plus economic reform) was suppressed in 1968 by direct military intervention. One cannot seriously consider Ceausescu's Romania other than as a crude despotism, politically reminiscent of Stalinism, and in economic trouble, contrasting with the less oppressive and economically more successful Bulgaria. Poland is a special case. Until the rise of Solidarity the Polish regime could be seen as a particularly notable example of an unrepresentative clique ruling over a basically disaffected people, committing major blunders of economic policy (e.g. the totally unsound boom of 1971–5) and unable to cope with its political consequences. Then in 1979–81 "solidarity" demonstrated to the world the hollowness of the claim that the system was in any conceivable way representative of the workers, of their aims or aspirations, though the claim that this is so (however hollow in fact) is an ideological imperative of the first order. The party was utterly demoralized, many members joined "Solidarity". So total was the party's paralysis that the suppression of "Solidarity", the restoration of "order", took the form of martial law, with a special role for professional army officers, a quite unprecedented turn of events. The special position of the Church is another feature peculiarly Polish. Furthermore, General Jaruzelski's government has now embarked upon an economic reform which, in its principles, is remarkably similar to that adopted in Hungary.

All these developments cannot but have some eventual influence on events in the Soviet Union itself, since there too one is witnessing what could be called a "crisis of system", a degree of economic malfunctioning which the new generation of leaders is being called upon to remedy. Failure to act may have serious consequences both within the Soviet Union and on its relations with (and influence upon) the world outside. Indeed, Gorbachev made this very point, in describing the need for economic reform: "the historic fate of our country, the position of socialism in the contemporary world, depends in large measure on how we tackle this task" (*Pravda,* 24 April 1985). And any remedy will inevitably involve action far removed from what Marx (and the Marxist tradition) had considered to be part of the transition to communism.

References

[1] Avtorkhanov, A. (1973), *Proiskhozheniye partokratii,* Frankfurt/Main, Posen.
[2] Bettelheim, C. (1982), *La Lutte des Classes en URSS,* vol. 3, Paris, Maspero/Seuil.

[3] Bienkowski, A. (1981), *Theory and Reality,* London, Allison & Busby.
[4] Brus, W. (1975), *Socialist Ownership and Political Systems,* London, Routledge and Kegan Paul.
[5] Brus, W. (1980), "Political System and Economic Efficiency", *Journal of Comparative Economics,* vol. **4,** n° 1, pp. 40–55.
[6] Bukharin, N. and Preobrazhensky, E. (1969), *The ABC of Communism,* Harmondworth, Penguin.
[7] Bukharin, N. (1921), *Teoriya istoricheskogo materializma, populyarny uchebnik marksistskoy sotsiologii,* Moscow.
[8] Bukharin, N. (1920), *Ekonomika perekhodnogo perioda, obshchya teoriya transformatsionnogo protsessa,* Moscow.
[9] Castoriadis, C. (1973), *La société bureaucratique,* Paris, Union Générale d'Editions.
[10] Chavance, B. (1981), June, "La nature du systeme soviétique", *Les temps modernes.*
[11] Chayanov ("Kremnev"), A. V. (1981), *Puteshestiviye moego brata Aleksiya v strane krastyanskoi utopii,* reprinted in New York (The "Utopia" was dated 1984!).
[12] Ciliga, C. (1979), *The Russian Enigma,* London, Ink Links (written in 1936).
[13] Danilova, L. V. (1958), in *Problemy istorii dokapitalisticheskikh obshchestv,* vol. 1, Moscow.
[14] Day, R. B. (1973), *Leon Trotsky and the Politics of Economic Isolation,* Cambridge, Cambridge University Press.
[15] Dmitrenko, V. (1974), "Stanovlennie kontsepsii razvitogo sotsializma v SSSR", *Voprosy istorii,* n° 8.
[16] Feher, F., Å. Heller, and G. Markus, (1983), *Dictatorship Over Needs,* Oxford, Basil Blackwell.
[17] Gouldner, A. W. (1980), *The Two Marxisms,* London, MacMillan.
[18] Grossman, V. (1970), *Vsyo techyot,* Frankfurt, Possev verlag.
[19] Harding, N. (ed.) (1984), *The State in Socialist Society,* London, Macmillan.
[20] Harding, N. (1977), *Lenin's Political Thoughts,* Vol. **1,** London, Macmillan.
[21] Heller, A. (1976), *The Theory of Need in Marx,* London, Allison & Busby.
[22] Hirszowicz, M. (1980), *The Bureaucratic Leviathan,* London, Martin Robinson.
[23] Jowitt, K. (1983), "Soviet Neotraditionalism: The Political Corruption of a Leninist Regime", *Soviet Studies,* vol. **35,** n° 3.
[24] Klenov, A., (pseud?), (1984), "Filosofiya neuverennosti", *Sintaksis,* n° 12.
[25] Kamenev, L., cited in [16].
[26] Konrad, G. and I. Szelenyi, (1979), *The Intellectuals on the Road to Class Power,* Brighton, Harvester Press.
[27] Kritsman, L. (1924), *Vestnik Kommunisticheskoi akademii,* n° 19.
[28] Lane, D. (1982), *The End of Social Inequality?,* London, Allen and Unwin.
[29] Lefort, C. (1971), *Elements d'une critique de la bureaucratie,* Genève/Paris, Droz.
[30] Lenin, V. (1964), *Sochineniya,* vol. **45,** Moscow, 5th edition.
[31] Luxemburg, R., cited from B. Knei-Paz, (1978), *The Social and Political Thought of Leon Trotsky,* Oxford, Clarendon Press.
[32] Luxemburg, R., cited from J. P. Nettl, (1966), *Rosa Luxemburg,* abridged edition, Oxford, Oxford University Press.
[33] Markus, C. (1980), "Planning the Crisis", *Praxis International,* n° 3.
[34] Marx, K. (1973), *Grundrisse: Foundations of the Critique of Political Economy,* Harmondworth, Penguin.
[35] Markovic, M. (1977), in R. C. Tucker, *Stalinism,* New York, Norton.

[36] McAuley, M., "The state in socialist society", in N. Harding [19].
[37] Nikiforov, V. (1984), "Teoria obshchestvennoi-ekonomicheskoi formatsii", *Voprosy istorii,* n° 8.
[38] Nove, A. (1969), "History, Hierarchy and Nationalities", *Soviet Studies,* Vol. **21,** n° 1.
[39] Olsevich, Y. (ed.), (1983), *Ekonomicheskoye razvitiye SSSR: kritika burzhuaznykh kontseptsii,* Moscow.
[40] Rakovsky, R. (1928), *Byulletin oppozitsii,* n° 6, and in C. Howe (ed.) 1976, *Essential Works of Socialism,* New Haven, Yale University Press.
[41] Shanin, T. (1983), *Late Marx and the Russian Road,* London, Routledge & Kegan Paul.
[42] Sochor, L. (1984), "Contribution of an Analysis of the Conservation Features of the Ideology of 'Real Socialism', in *Research Project on Crises in Soviet-type Systems,* study n° 4.
[43] Selucky, R. (1979), *Marxism, Socialism and Freedom,* London, MacMillan.
[44] Shturman, D. (1981), *Nash novyi mir,* Jerusalem, Lexicon.
[45] Trotsky, L. D. (1975), *The Challenge of the Left Opposition, 1923–1925,* New York, Pathfinder Press.
[46] Trotsky, L. D. (1925), *Sochineniya,* vol. **12,** Moscow.
[47] Trotsky, L. D. (1932), (1933), cited from *Byulletin oppozitsii,* n° 31 and n° 34.
[48] Utechin, S. V. (1963), *Russian Political Thought,* New York, F. A. Praeger.
[49] Wittfogel, K. (1957), *Oriental Despotism,* New Haven, Yale University Press.
[50] Voslensky, M. (1980), *La Nomenclatura,* Paris, Pierre Belfond.
[51] XYZ (Anonymous), (1929–30), cited in *Byulletin oppozitsii,* n° 15/16 and n° 17/18.

INDEX

For Product Safety Concerns and Information please contact our EU
representative GPSR@taylorandfrancis.com
Taylor & Francis Verlag GmbH, Kaufingerstraße 24, 80331 München, Germany

www.ingramcontent.com/pod-product-compliance
Ingram Content Group UK Ltd
Pitfield, Milton Keynes, MK11 3LW, UK
UKHW022108190926
475702UK00013B/1330
9780415866149